LANGSTON HUGHES
A Biography

LANGSTON HUGHES

HUGHES
A Biography

BY MILTON MELTZER

Thomas Y. Crowell   New York

Acknowledgment is made to the following publishers for permission to reprint
copyrighted material:

Hill & Wang, Inc., for excerpts from *The Big Sea* by Langston Hughes, copyright
1940 by Langston Hughes.

Alfred A. Knopf, Inc., for "Bound North Blues" and "Homesick Blues" from *The
Dream Keeper* by Langston Hughes, copyright 1932 by Alfred A. Knopf, Inc.;
"Border Line," "Cross," "I, Too, Sing America," and "The Weary Blues" from
Selected Poems by Langston Hughes, copyright © 1959 by Langston Hughes;
and "Christ in Alabama" from *The Panther and the Lash* copyright © 1967 by
Langston Hughes.

By the Author

A PICTORIAL HISTORY OF THE NEGRO IN AMERICA
(*with Langston Hughes*)

A LIGHT IN THE DARK:
The Life of Samuel Gridley Howe

TONGUE OF FLAME:
The Life of Lydia Maria Child

IN THEIR OWN WORDS:
A History of the American Negro
Volume I 1619–1865
Volume II 1865–1916
Volume III 1916–1966

THADDEUS STEVENS AND THE FIGHT FOR NEGRO RIGHTS

BLACK MAGIC:
A Pictorial History of the Negro in American Entertainment
(*with Langston Hughes*)

LANGSTON HUGHES—A BIOGRAPHY

Contents

Contents

Introduction

Good writing, Langston Hughes believed, comes out of your own life. You start at home, with what you know best—your own family, your ne ghbor-hood, your city. One of the first things he remem-bered from childhood was a voice on Independence Avenue in Kansas City. It was singing the blues.

He tried early to capture on paper the sound of the blues. It was a hard thing to do, working with words alone. But he learned how and his first book of poems was *The Weary Blues*. He was twenty-four years old then, and it was already plain that he had mastered a lesson he would offer young writers many years later. "You have to learn to be yourself," he said, "natural and undeceived as to who you are, calmly and surely you."

To start with what he was: an American, and

black. Except for the Indians, every American is a hyphenate, beginning with the Anglo-Americans who landed at Jamestown and Plymouth Rock. But for the Afro-American, who came here just as early, life in the land where "white is right" has always been different.

It is that difference which Langston Hughes' poetry illuminates. He voiced the condition of the black American. He listened closely, and heard; he saw, and understood; he touched, and felt; he knew, and remembered. Within a few years of his first book, he was the poet laureate of his people. Their life was his life, and he wrote about it as it was. He was a poet first, but he used every form—the short story, novel, play, song, musical comedy, opera, history, humor, autobiography. At the end, the shelf of his published work ran over forty volumes and with it should be included his many recordings, radio and television scripts, and hundreds of columns and articles for newspapers and magazines. It was a staggering production for a man who never seemed to be in a hurry.

One of the last times I saw him was in the spring of 1967. It was a warm Saturday afternoon. The stoops of the Harlem tenements were full of gossiping men and women; 127th Street was jumping with children's games. Near one end of the block was a storefront church; and at the far end, toward Lenox Avenue, a big new public school turned windowless brick walls to the neighborhood.

Number 20, where Langston lived, is a three-story brownstone, much like the old houses that crowd it in. The only difference was the plot of ground beside the stoop. It was hardly a yard square, but Langston had put a garden in. At first the kids had stepped all over the greenery. He got around that the next spring by calling them in to help with the planting. He had each one print his name on a stake to show where he had sown. The garden came up safe, with nasturtiums and marigolds and asters blooming all summer.

Up two flights of steep stairs, at the top of the house was his workroom. It was a good-sized rectangle, the two long walls lined from floor to ceiling with books. At the end of the room, between the two tall windows that looked out over Harlem's roofs, was a big T-shaped desk. Filing cabinets stood within reach of the chair and typewriter. On top of the desk were scattered piles of books and folders and manuscript sheets and letters and magazines and clippings. Langston wore an old pair of pants and slippers, and a striped sport shirt opened wide for comfort. It was after two, but he was just finishing breakfast. It was his habit to start work after midnight, getting to bed at dawn, and sleeping through the morning. In those hours he would be sure not to be interrupted by calls or visitors.

He did not get along very well on less than eight hours sleep. Ten hours suited him better, and twelve hours, he would say, "really restores my soul." He liked nothing better than to sleep—unless it was to eat, a characteristic noticed early. (His high-school yearbook announced, in a section headed "Little-Known Facts About Well-Known People": "Langston Hughes is crazy about eats.")

He poured coffee, pushing aside the pile of unread mail that had arrived that morning. He leaned back in his chair, his hands folded over the paunch that had bulged in recent years, his eyes bright and warm behind the glasses. The talk moved from humorous criticism of an experimental play he'd seen the night before to what he himself was working on now. The never-absent cigarette dangled from his lip, the ashes tumbling down over his shirt as he talked.

Getting up, he pulled together several folders lying about on shelves or the desk. Here were the galley proofs of a new book of poems due out in the fall, the drafts of liner notes for an album of folk music, a pile of photos of paintings for an art book whose text he was planning to write, a tentative list of chapter headings for his projected book of memoirs of Harlem.

It was a terrifying mountain of work to think of attacking. Didn't he ever intend to take it easy? Not hardly, he said. He hoped to be writing for a long time. He liked it, and he thought he was lucky to be able to make a living from something he liked doing. What could be better than working for yourself, with nobody telling you what to do or how to do it? Living this way it was impossible to be bored or tired. Then he began trying out some of the lines he had thought up as a starting point for a book of new cartoons to illustrate the special quality of Negro humor.

He was sixty-five now. But you didn't think of him as of any particular age. He was simply himself, the kind of man who must have been there always for all of us who need someone like him. He would last, if anything in life would. It was a quiet durability he had, like some element deep in the earth that powerful pressures had not fractured or scarred, but had made into a glowing diamond.

1 *Wandering*

How do people become poets? To hear him tell it, it was not his own decision but his classmates' that started Langston Hughes writing poems. He was about to graduate from grammar school in Lincoln, Illinois. The students had elected all their officers except the class poet. It stumped them because none of them had ever written a poem. One thing they had learned, however: a good poem has rhythm. And like most white Americans, they believed all Negroes have rhythm, too. So when someone yelled out his name, the vote went unanimously to Langston.

He was fourteen then. He had never thought of being a writer but he did not refuse the honor. He went home and wrote sixteen verses in praise of the teachers and his class.

Langston Hughes enjoyed telling this story about the odd beginning of a poet. He liked to leave the impression that if he hadn't been applauded at graduation that might have been not only his first but his last poem. But class election or not, it is altogether likely that he would have started writing poetry soon enough. There is his own evidence for it. In the same place where he told of hearing the wandering musicians playing guitars and singing the blues in Kansas City, he said that "some of my earliest attempts at verse-making were creating words in my own mind to the rhythms of the blues." But he did not put the words down. Most of us try to make poems sometime in our life, especially when we're young. It's when we grow older that something gets tight inside and we begin to resist poetry.

Why didn't that happen to Langston? There was his own nature, to begin with, and the influences of his family. His father was James Nathaniel Hughes and his mother, Carrie Mercer Langston. They brought a richly mixed set of ancestors together in their son. Both his paternal great-grandfathers were white, and both from Kentucky. One had been a Jewish slave trader and the other, of Scotch descent, was engaged in the more respectable business of making whiskey. The distiller was said to be related to Henry Clay, the famed Senator.

On his mother's side there was great-grandfather Ralph Quarles, a white Virginia planter, who claimed ancestry from the seventeenth-century English poet Francis Quarles. By his slave housekeeper, Lucy Langston, Ralph Quarles had four children. One of these was Langston's grandfather, Charles Langston, and another was the great-uncle who became a Congressman, John Mercer Langston. There was French and Indian blood on that side, too, going back to a French trader who had come down from Canada to the Carolinas and married a Cherokee girl.

It was in Joplin, a little Missouri town, that Langston Hughes began life on February 1, 1902. While Langston was still a baby, James Hughes, an angry dark-brown man, walked out of the house one day, leaving his wife and son behind, and headed south. He didn't stop running until he reached Mexico.

It was color that drove James Hughes out of his country. He had studied to become a lawyer. But when he asked to take the examination for the bar, he had been told No—Negroes are not allowed. It was the last blow from a Jim Crow society that denied his right to live. Some, facing the same barriers, gave up and sank into bitter silence. In others the fires of anger burst out into passionate protest. For James Hughes, the way out was escape, flight, self-exile. And in him, as his son would learn later, the bitterness became bile that ate away whatever pride in his people he may once have known. From hating his oppressor he turned to hating himself and his color.

Left alone with a baby, Carrie Langston had a hard time. She had studied at the University of Kansas, but for any woman, and a Negro woman especially, finding a good job was not easy. She moved from place to place, now out of work, now hoping to find something a little better. Sometimes she kept her boy with her, but often she couldn't hold down a job and take care of Langston, too. When it came time for him to start school, his mother had a job as stenographer to a Negro lawyer in Topeka, the capital of Kansas. There was a fair-sized Negro community there, the families of freedmen who had streamed up from the South around 1880 to look for a better life in the state John Brown had fought to make free. The "exodusters," as they were called, had found no promised land. Nor was it any better now. Mrs. Hughes could find a room only in a business block, over a plumber's shop. A little one-pot stove did for cooking and heating. To keep it going little Langston scoured the alleys behind the stores for discarded boxes.

When fall came his mother took Langston to the nearest school. It turned out to be for whites only. The school officials sent him away. Kansas wasn't South, but it was Jim Crow just the same. Across the railroad tracks is the colored school, they said: You belong there. Mrs. Hughes did not agree. She was a fighter, and she took her case right to the school board. She kept arguing and pestering till she won, and Langston by himself desegregated the Harrison Street School.

Perhaps because he was the only Negro child, the teachers didn't mind this small token of desegregation. Except for one. Looking at Langston, she felt she had to tell the class she just didn't like colored people. Sometimes her spoken meanness led her pupils to chase Langston home, flinging tin cans and stones at the five-year-old as he ran down the alleys. They weren't all like that. One white boy always stood by him, and sometimes others defended him too.

In those days, before the movies, people relied

on traveling theater companies for entertainment. Mrs. Hughes liked to see plays. One of the first shows she took Langston to see was *Uncle Tom's Cabin,* the dramatization of Harriet Beecher Stowe's famous antislavery novel. Because his mother liked to read, too, books early became something for the boy to enjoy with her. He was even introduced to art at first hand, for right in the next room was a young Negro painter whose eye was fixed not on Topeka but on some far Africa of his dreams. When Langston stepped through the painter's door he entered a world of brilliant lions and tigers roaming a canvas jungle.

Missing each other, his mother and father decided to go back together again. Mr. Hughes sent for his family, and they came down to Mexico City. Almost the moment they arrived a great earthquake shook the city. Buildings caved in, great holes yawned in the earth, and tarantulas crawled out of the walls. Mrs. Hughes could not have been very sure of her feelings about her husband, for this was enough to turn her around. Kansas was for her, not this Mexico, where people did not speak any language she could understand and where you might disappear into the ground you stood on. For six-year-old Langston, Mexico meant only a strange man called

"father" carrying him in his arms the night the
earth rocked and roared.

They were not back in Kansas very long when
Mrs. Hughes decided to put Langston in her
mother's care. Only seven now, and left without
mother or father, this could have been a terrible
time for the boy. But he was lucky in his grandmother, Mary Langston. She was a remarkable
woman. Everyone said he looked like her, with his
copper-brown skin, and his straight, black hair. She
looked like an Indian to Langston, which was natural, for her own grandmother had been a Cherokee
of North Carolina. Mary Langston had been born
free during slavery days, and had been able to cross
into the free state of Ohio. There she had been the
first Negro woman to attend Oberlin College.
While at Oberlin, she met Lewis Sheridan Leary, a
fugitive slave who had also come from North
Carolina. Leary was a young saddle and harness
maker who had come to know John Brown, the
abolitionist, then living in Ohio. Mary and Lewis
were married. One day he said he had to leave on
a trip, but did not say where he was going. A few
weeks passed, and then the news exploded on front
pages from one end of the country to the other:
John Brown and his band of twenty-one men had

attacked the federal arsenal at Harpers Ferry in Virginia. Their goal was to take the town, put arms in the hands of the slaves, and carry the revolt deep into the South. In the small army were five Negroes. One of them, the papers said, was Lewis Sheridan Leary. Badly wounded in the action, he lived only eight hours more. Back to his young widow in Ohio came all that was left of her husband—his shawl, full of bullet holes.

Mary never regretted marrying a man ready to die for his people's freedom. She proved it by marrying another man who took the same risks for the same cause. His name was Charles Langston. Only a year before the John Brown raid, he had joined other men in forcibly taking from United States marshals a fugitive slave they had seized near Oberlin. Indicted and convicted for breaking the Fugitive Slave Law, Charles Langston went to jail. But it did not worry him. "The Fugitive Slave Law was made to be broken," the abolitionists said.

In the 1870s, when the migration movement to Kansas was under way, Charles and Mary Langston joined it. There, on a farm near Lawrence, Langston's mother was born. The Civil War had been fought and the Emancipation Proclamation had been won. But Charles Langston didn't give himself over to making money. It didn't interest him; freedom did. He thought the ending of slavery was only a beginning. Black Americans were still denied equality, in the North as well as the South. And freedom without equality was the shell without the egg. He had a farm and a grocery store in Lawrence but gave most of his time to the political struggle for equal rights. The family was usually broke. When Charles Langston died, there wasn't any money left to support his family.

Somehow Mary Langston got along on her own. When young Langston came to live with her in Lawrence she was about seventy. That was a very ancient age in the eyes of a boy of seven.

It was a bleak, lonesome time. What made it worse was their poverty. His grandmother had a fierce pride. She would not work for anyone else. The only jobs open to black women were chores for whites—cooking, cleaning, washing. She would not go into their homes to do their work.

Instead, she tried to make a living by renting rooms to students at the nearby University of Kansas. Sometimes half the little house was taken over by a family. And sometimes she and the boy moved out to live with a friend while the whole house was occupied by renters. Even with that, she got no more than ten or twelve dollars a month for it. There was little to eat on that income. Salt pork and wild dandelions—he often had to make a meal out of that. What money came in had to go to interest payments on the mortgage. They lived under the constant threat of losing the roof over their heads.

Hard as these times were, Mary Langston would not beg or borrow. She was like granite that troubles could not wear away. It was a toughness—but not a hardness—she could never be like that—Langston had to learn early. Lawrence was another lesson in Jim Crow, just as Topeka had been—Topeka, where the corner drugstore would sell his mother soap but would not let Langston buy an ice-cream soda because it meant sitting down at the counter.

There were no nickels or dimes to spare for the movie theater that had opened in Lawrence. But even if there had been, a sign outside read: COLORED NOT ADMITTED.

It was like that at school. Langston was in the second grade now, but he was not studying in the same room with the other second-graders. He was steered to another room, where he found himself

sitting with children from six different grades. The
reason was plain: they were all black.

And it was the same again when it came to school
sports. He could not enter the track meets or the
swimming races. The YMCA next to the school,
which the students used for showers and swimming,
would not admit Negro children. Young Men's
Christian Association, he thought. Is that what it
means?

He found out early that what was happening to
himself wasn't anything unique or special. He could
read now, and there every week in the Topeka *Plain
Dealer,* the Negro newspaper his grandmother took,
were great big headlines that scared him half to
death. Beatings, whippings, jailings, lynchings. How
could anyone dare go down South? You might be
lynched the minute you stepped off the train, he
thought. Even in the days when nothing had happened to him, he knew from the papers what white
folks had just done to other black folks.

But he knew, too, that Negroes defended themselves, fought back, yelled and hollered and organized. His grandmother was teaching him. They
had each other for comfort in those lonely days.
Summer evenings on the front porch they sat to-

gether, talking. She was tall and straight in her rocker, her long black hair graying only a little, her eyes steady and clear in her copper face. Langston would sit on a little stool next to her, leaning against her legs. Or he would be stretched out on the floor, staring up at the stars sparkling in the night, while she told him stories. They were always about freedom, and they went back all the way to slavery times. Her father, a free Negro, had helped slaves in North Carolina by taking them on as apprentice stonemasons and, when they had earned the money to buy their freedom from their owners, he had helped them go North to where there was no slavery.

One of his earliest memories was of the time his grandmother took him to hear Booker T. Washington. He was probably seven then. With his grandmother he climbed the hill to the university. The hall was crowded. He had never seen so many Negroes and whites together. He gathered from the talk around him that some kind of controversy surrounded Mr. Washington. When the great man came onto the platform he was seated in the center of all the white men. Langston had never before seen a colored man the center of attention. At the end there was a great burst of applause. He couldn't re-

member a word Booker T. had said, probably because he understood little, if anything, of the speech.
"But I was very proud that a man of my own color
was the center of all this excitement."

When Langston was eight, his grandmother took
him to Osawatomie, where President Theodore
Roosevelt was dedicating a monument to old John
Brown. Langston saw his grandmother seated on
the platform, and honored as the last of the widows
of the men who had tried to shatter slavery at
Harpers Ferry.

John Brown, Frederick Douglass, David Walker,
Nat Turner, Harriet Tubman—she knew what they
had said and done, and in those growing years she
saw that Langston knew, too. The stories she told
Langston were always about heroes. The men and
women in them never cried. They worked and
planned and fought, and often they lost. But they
never cried. It was her way of teaching the boy the
uselessness of tears. If life hurt you, she seemed to
be telling him, don't turn from it. Meet it and fight
to make it what you want.

She shared with him a magazine called *The Crisis.*
It was a thin monthly full of pictures of prominent
Negroes and stories about race activities all over
the country. The first beautiful and moving words

Langston remembered had been the passages from the Bible his grandmother read to him. Now he heard other words that moved him, in a voice sounding from the pages of *The Crisis,* the passionate words of Dr. William Edward Burghardt Du Bois, its editor.

The magazine spoke for an organization that had recently been founded, the National Association for the Advancement of Colored People. It had risen out of the ashes of Springfield, Illinois, where a white mob had raged through the streets of Lincoln's town for two days, looting and burning Negro homes, lynching two men, injuring scores of others, and driving hundreds out of the city. It was nothing new in America—only the latest example of mob violence that had brought more than a thousand lynchings in the first ten years of this twentieth century.

Why Negroes and whites joined together in the NAACP was made plain in *The Crisis:*

> To promote equality of rights and eradicate caste or race prejudice among the citizens of the United States; to advance the interests of colored citizens; to secure for them impartial suffrage; and to increase their opportunities for securing justice in

the courts, education for their children, employment according to their ability, and complete equality before the law.

Dr. Du Bois is a great man, Langston's grandmother said, a doctor of philosophy educated at Harvard and in European universities, too. But he's not great just because he's educated. He's great because he wants us to have our rights. He believes in equality and he fights for it.

It was a book by this same Du Bois that Langston treasured most as a boy. Not because it was the first book he had come across. He had discovered the world of books earlier, when his mother had taken him to the small library on the grounds of the state capitol in Topeka. He loved the ivy greening the walls, the cool quiet inside, the roomy chairs, and the big tables. And the librarians—those warm, gentle women who had time to talk to a small boy and help him find wonderful books.

These were children's books with lovely pictures to look at, and poems and stories that librarians or his mother would read to him. They were about worlds you could escape into, where people ate all they wanted and didn't worry about losing their homes to the bank.

The book by Dr. Du Bois was different. It was called *The Souls of Black Folk.* The sentences drove straight at you. They made you think hard about the strange meaning of being black here and now.

"The problem of the twentieth century is the problem of the color line."

Again and again Mary Langston read those words from the very first page of the book to her grandson. And then: "How does it feel to be a problem?" A strange experience, Du Bois went on, peculiar even for one who has never been anything else from babyhood. When Du Bois described how the shadow of color had first swept over him as a schoolboy in the Berkshire Hills, Langston knew what he was writing about—the sudden realization that, much as you felt like others in your heart and longings, you were different, "shut out from their world by a vast veil."

As he listened to the words of Du Bois, and read them for himself, he began to understand many things about racism: how it had arisen, whose interests it served, what it had done to both black and white. Du Bois could help him to understand what was shaping within himself:

One ever feels his two-ness—an American, a

Negro; two souls, two thoughts, two unreconciled strivings; two warring ideals in one dark body, whose dogged strength alone keeps it from being torn asunder.

The history of the American Negro is the history of this strife—this longing to attain self-conscious manhood, to merge his double self into a better and truer self. In this merging he wishes neither of the old selves to be lost. He would not Africanize America, for America has too much to teach the world and Africa. He would not bleach his Negro soul in a flood of white Americanism, for he knows that Negro blood has a message for the world. He simply wishes to make it possible without being cursed and spit upon by his fellows, for a man to be both a Negro and an American, without having the doors of opportunity closed roughly in his face.

His grandmother died when Langston was twelve. It was the first time he had faced the death of someone so close to him. Seven years later he would write a loving poem about "old Aunt Sue" with "a whole heart full of stories" about black people, and a quiet, dark-faced child she tells them to, during summer nights on the front porch.

2

Brass
Spittoons

Friends of his grandmother took Langston in when her death left him alone. He called them Auntie and Uncle Reed. The Reeds had a house in Lawrence close by the Kaw River, and owned it outright; there was no mortgage hanging overhead. Uncle Reed had steady work with the city, digging ditches and laying sewer pipes. Auntie Reed took care of the chickens and cows in their backyard and sold eggs and milk to the neighbors. At their table Langston could stuff himself with Auntie's fine salt pork and greens, fresh peas and young onions right out of the garden, followed by hoecake and apple dumplings washed down with cool, creamy milk.

He helped by setting hens and driving the cows

to pasture. He carried in the water for the washtub, chopped the wood and piled it behind the stove, and ran errands to the store. But he wanted to earn some money of his own. The first pennies came in from collecting maple seeds in springtime and selling them to the seed store. He delivered papers, too, and sold *The Saturday Evening Post.* He became a real wage earner when he found a job in an old hotel near his school. Every afternoon when classes were over, he went to the back door of the hotel and stowed his books in the closet that held the brooms and cleaning rags. He swept the halls and stairways and the lobby, dusted the chairs, and cleaned the toilets. Then he picked up the big brass spittoons, dumped their slime into the alley, rinsed them out and polished them till they glittered like gold. By six o'clock the run-down lobby looked a little better, and the six brass bowls sparkled in the glow of the electric lamps. The next day, when he came to work, the bowls were filthy again with gum and tobacco juice and cigarette butts and spit.

It was a small hotel, and not a nice one. There were just two bellboys, old men now, and Langston found both had started young there—at about the same age he was—and had grown up on the job.

What went on in the hotel puzzled him sometimes, but he didn't ask any questions, and nobody told him anything.

Sometimes he ran errands for the boss, and shined shoes for men sitting in the lobby chairs. When he was polishing the spittoons, his mind would float off. He thought about school and what he might do when he was a man. How did people get to be great? What could you do to make yourself great? He wondered what his mother and father were doing, one way down in Mexico, the other off somewhere in Illinois, and if they wanted him with them. He wished he had a brother. He could talk to him about things and not have to think to himself so much. When he got married, he'd have a lot of children. They wouldn't have to grow up lonesome.

The hotel paid Langston fifty cents a week. With it he went to the movies. He liked Charlie Chaplin's comedies and those thriller serials in which the heroine was always about to be strangled or run over by a train when the episode ended. Then one day a sign went up over the box office: NO COLORED ADMITTED. He took his fifty cents elsewhere, buying a seat way up at the top of the Opera House gallery—Negroes couldn't sit anywhere else—to see the kind of road show his mother used to take him to.

Saturday afternoons in the fall he watched the football games in the big university stadium. Unwittingly the university provided him with another, and a gruesome, form of entertainment. Because he was a small boy, nobody paid any attention to him when he sneaked into the medical school building. He would hide off in a corner and watch the students dissect corpses. He was fascinated by it, and even amused, but somehow never horrified.

Churchgoing was a regular necessity for Auntie Reed, and she insisted that Langston go to church and Sunday school. She couldn't order Uncle Reed around, however, and that sinner spent his Sunday mornings at home, washing his overalls and peacefully puffing his pipe.

In Sunday school the old lady teacher used colored picture cards with a printed text to explain about the Bible. Jesus was the color of the white folks that all the black folks in town cooked and scrubbed and cleaned for. His long, straight blond hair swept down over the shoulders of His white gown. All the saints wore robes like that on the Sunday school cards, and he wondered if they wore pants underneath or what. And why did they wear their hair so long? And how could the angels with those long, long wings ever sit down? But they were always standing or flying on the cards, never sitting.

When the children sang "Jesus Wants Me for a Sunbeam," Langston's mind would drift off to pictures of a white God listening. Did he care about black folks? Did he know Langston was sitting there in Sunday school this minute wondering what kind of drawers Jesus wore?

Lawrence had only two colored churches (Negroes then didn't dream of going to a white church), a Baptist and a Methodist. Langston had been christened in the Methodist church, which drew mostly middle-class people, but he liked Auntie Reed's Baptists best. During revival time at her church the preaching and praying, singing and shouting would go on every night for weeks. "When the Saints Go Marching In" and "That Old Time Religion" rocked the walls as the worshipers, heads back, and feet and hands beating rhythm, repeated choruses again and again. Floods of melody rolled up under the roof and almost lifted it off.

More and more sinners were brought to Jesus as the nights rocked on. Toward the end, one night was reserved for children, and Langston was put up front on the mourners' bench with the other "young lambs" who had not yet come into the fold.

The preacher prayed, half-chanting, half-moaning the rhythmical sentences, stretching his arms wide to draw up the young sinners in the front row. The whole congregation wrestled for their souls, but although all the other girls and boys went up to the altar one by one and were saved, Langston couldn't feel the spirit in him. At last he rose, ashamed, and perhaps afraid to be alone, and pretended to be like the others. The whole church, Auntie Reed leading them, sang his praises. But it was a lie, and in bed that night, alone with it, he cried himself to sleep.

3 *Homesick Blues*

From Auntie Reed's window Langston could see the trains shoot past, almost leaping the bridge over the brown-gold river, pouring out a great cloud of smoke and cinders that hid the wheat fields. He used to walk down to the station and stare up the tracks, wondering what Chicago was like at the other end. To every boy in Kansas that was the biggest city, a dream of a place you hoped to see for yourself some day. Walking on the railroad ties, he would think about Auntie and Uncle Reed. He loved them very much. They had taken him in and were caring for him while his mother was moving around from one place to another and his father was down in Mexico. He shut his eyes and unreeled a little movie he had made up about his father. He was a big bronze cow-boy in a dashing sombrero, riding a powerful black horse somewhere in the mountains of Mexico. The sun was burning down on him and the horse's hooves kicked up the dust between the cacti. He smiled at Langston as he galloped past. *He's* free, the boy thought, free of white folks and their color craziness. He didn't know when he would see his father again, if ever. . . . Know what I am? A passed-around boy. The phrase amused him. But it was true. He was always being left with whoever was willing to take care of him. Not that anyone had been mean to him. No. After all, he had a house to live in, and people to live with. And they loved him. But it wasn't the same as belonging to somebody who would say, "You're mine," and it would be true, really true. He had the "Homesick Blues":

> De railroad bridge's
> A sad song in de air.
> De railroad bridge's
> A sad song in de air.
> Ever time de trains pass
> I wants to go somewhere.
> Homesick blues, Lawd,
> 'S a terrible thing to have.

25

Homesick blues is
A terrible thing to have.
To keep from cryin'
I opens ma mouth an' laughs.

He was going on fourteen when his mother finally sent for him. She had married again. Her husband was Homer Clarke, and they had settled down in Lincoln, a small town in the middle of Illinois. Langston liked his stepfather a lot, and now he had a young foster brother, named Gwyn. Maybe this was going to be the end of growing up lonesome.

But soon he found this family, too, would be broken up again and again. His stepfather was a cook, but he wasn't young any more, and he couldn't stand the heat of the kitchens. He had to look for other jobs. There was nothing easy for an older man to do, it seemed—coal mines, steel mills—and often he couldn't find work nearby and had to leave his family to look somewhere else.

Langston was going on with grammar school, a small one in Lincoln, with only eight teachers. His favorite was Miss Ethel Welsh. The best part of school, as always, was the reading it led to. Stories were what Langston liked most. The Westerns, especially, by Harold Bell Wright and Zane Grey, he couldn't get enough of.

Poems didn't interest him much. There were only two poets he liked, Longfellow (*Hiawatha* was a good story, after all), and Paul Laurence Dunbar. The son of former slaves, Dunbar had grown up in the Midwest, too. He had run elevators as a boy and even after he published his early poems. His first book had come out when he was only twenty-one. He had begun writing verse while still in grammar school. His poems about Negro farm folk were tender and funny, full of affection for his people. Many were in dialect. They had a swing and a beat Langston enjoyed.

Langston's mother wrote verse too, occasionally. More often she liked to recite poems—the longer the better, it seemed. She would dress up in costume to present them on church programs.

Once she draped Langston and another boy in sheets so they would look like the sons of Cornelia, a great lady of ancient Rome. These were her "jewels," the poem went, about to be torn away from her by a cruel fate. People packed the church to hear her recite the dramatic poem. But Langston didn't like it at all. In the middle of her recital, he began to roll his eyes wildly from side to side, as though he were suffering terribly. The audience smiled, then giggled, then laughed. As his mother went at her lines all the harder, Langston mugged all the harder. The audience laughed louder and louder. His mother couldn't imagine what was wrong, but she struggled on until the end, when there was an explosion of laughter that filled the church.

That cost Langston the hardest whipping his mother ever gave him. "I learned to respect other people's art," he said.

He had a chance to try his own hand at art when graduation time came round. It was then, upon being elected class poet, that he wrote his first poem.

4 *Central High*

Just when Langston finished grammar school his stepfather found a job in a steel mill in Cleveland. Homer Clarke was making good money now and the family left Illinois to join him in Ohio. The great war that had begun in Europe in 1914 had opened up jobs for Negroes in America by cutting off the flood of immigration. The factories, straining to meet war orders from abroad, were short of unskilled workers. They began hiring Negroes. By the tens of thousands Negroes trained up from the South to fill the jobs. Chicago, New York, Philadelphia, Pittsburgh, Detroit, Cleveland—big industrial centers all—looked like the Promised Land to sharecroppers and tenant farmers. Living a kind of semi-slavery in the South, they wanted freedom, a place where they could work, a decent home, and schools their children could go to.

There was work in Cleveland all right. The giant steel mills fanning out from the shore of Lake Erie were booming. And it was hard work, Mr. Clarke found. Every day he had to put in several hours' overtime. It meant extra money, but after a while Langston noticed he had changed, aged, seemed drained away. Finally he couldn't take the heat of the furnaces any more. He got a job as a janitor of an apartment house.

The east side of Cleveland was jammed tight with the new arrivals. It was very hard for Negroes to find a place to live. Through all his years at high school Langston's family was never able to live in anything but a basement or an attic. And they had to pay a lot for it, too.

The landlords cut up the old houses into small apartments, packing in five or six families where one used to live, and charging each family as much as the whites had paid for the whole house. Sheds, garages, stores—every empty place was turned into living quarters. It was the same for Negroes in all the big cities. Whole sections became black ghettoes as whites refused to live in the same neighborhood with blacks.

The high rents took most of the wages blacks earned. There was no escape into a home of your own, for the banks and real-estate people refused to sell, or else set very hard terms. Langston's mother took a job as a maid to help meet expenses. When she paid another woman to take care of his little brother, there wasn't much left.

Central High School, where Langston went, reflected the changes in Cleveland. Once, long ago, it had been the school for wealthy whites. When they moved farther out, the poor whites and the children of the foreign-born moved in. By the time Langston entered, the students were mostly the children of people from forty-eight different nations with some Negroes mixed in. (Later the school became almost all Negro.)

Slim, handsome, with an easy laugh, Langston made friends early at high school. They called him "Lang."

His schoolmates recall that he cropped his hair close and dressed conservatively. He had none of the self-conscious mannerisms that adolescents sometimes assume to call attention to themselves. Although he was interested in the arts and was a good student, he was neither arty nor given to flights of highbrow talk or flashy class recitations, a friend said. Never gloomy or moody, his quiet natural ways made the whole school his friends. Without trying for it, he was recognized as a school leader. "Everyone adored him," Henry Kraus remembers.

Langston tried out for the track team. He was good in the high jump and the dash and his 440-yard relay team won the citywide championship twice. He went around the school sporting a sweater decorated with his athletic letter and club pins.

Most of the white students were Catholic or Jewish. They got along pretty well, except for class elections. Then there would be a split along religious lines, and in the deadlock Langston, the popular Protestant, was sometimes chosen for a class or club office as a compromise candidate. He did not seek honors or attention, but he was elected to Student Council, and was president of the American Civics Association, secretary of the French Club, and treasurer of the Home Garden Club.

Fun was centered around the school, for most of the students lived long streetcar distances away. Once home, they had little chance after studying to see friends. The after-school clubs, rehearsals, dances, and athletics kept many together. And always there was the endless talk, in which you discovered yourself and your friends. Langston's staff work on *The Monthly* was one center of his school life, and the Garden Club another. His greatest thrill came when he acted as special host to Noble Sissle, the Central alumnus who teamed with Eubie Blake to play their jazz music on both the white and Negro vaudeville circuits. Every time the duo reached Cleveland in those years and Sissle came over to play at a school assembly, Langston was happier than he had ever been.

But in his first year at Central he became part of a bigger community outside the school, a community so important to him that he would never stop coming back to it. To the middle of his neighborhood, the "Roaring Third," a young couple, Russell and Rowena Jelliffe, came in 1915 to begin settlement-house work. Midwesterners themselves, and classmates at Oberlin College, they had worked at Hull House in the slums of Chicago. They came to Cleveland at the invitation of the Second Presbyterian Church to build a community center for the thousands of black and white people newly arrived to

33

work in the factories. They named their settlement Karamu House, choosing a Swahili word that means both "community center" and "place of enjoyment."

Karamu opened around the corner from his house the year Langston moved to Cleveland, and he was one of the first youngsters to drift in. It was just two little frame cottages then, with the Jelliffes living in the rear one. The young social workers were wise enough to put their theories behind them and to learn from the community. Their program was shaped by the people who came to them, and Langston was one of them. They watched and interpreted as honestly as they could the unfolding of each child, looking for the things that would meet his basic needs. Langston did not talk about writing then; it was the graphic arts that he plunged into. Karamu had skilled teachers and he drew and painted under their eye. As he learned, he began helping others. Soon he was a volunteer, teaching block printing to a group of children.

The Jelliffes, like everyone else, could not help noticing his gaiety, his fine sense of humor, his sensitivity to beauty, his deep liking for people. "The outstanding thing to see," they said later, "was his wonder at the world. It shone through his deep hurt and his struggle to understand." They would come in late at night sometimes and find him asleep over their books in their living room. Once he eagerly invited them to his house to see Lewis Leary's shawl with the bullet holes, the shawl he had worn when he fell beside John Brown at Harpers Ferry.

Karamu, integrated from the beginning, developed a serious arts program as its means of opening avenues of understanding, cooperation, and friendship. To young Negroes like Langston it offered a chance to shape and express their experience, and for the talented, encouragement to pursue a career in the arts with some hope there would be less opposition than in other fields.

At school Langston's best friend was a tall, lively Polish boy who had two rosy-cheeked sisters and a mother who stuffed Langston with wonderful cabbage cooked in sweetened vinegar. They were a jolly and devout Catholic family who always made him feel at home. He had many friends among the Jewish students, too. They took him to their synagogue nearby the school a few times. Once he went to a big prayer meeting for the Polish Jews killed in a pogrom, and saw the old men striking their heads in sorrow against the walls. He went to hear his first symphony concert with a Jewish girl. He found that, in contrast to the native white boys and girls in the Kansas towns, these hard-working children of foreign-born parents were more democratic and less anti-Negro. Their interests were broader, too. They lent him books, introduced him to the new and radical ideas of the *Liberator* magazine, and took him to hear lectures.

Once the speaker was Eugene V. Debs, the Socialist leader who drew a great crowd into the Public Square. Debs was against America's getting into the war and he let everybody know it. He thought that both sides—the Germans and the Allies—were wrong, and that the war was unjust. But feeling for the war mounted, and many people got hysterical about anyone who opposed it. In Cleveland, the police raided the homes of several of Langston's classmates, and took all their books away. With many other students, Langston was called down to the principal's office. What kind of an American, the principal asked, would go to a Debs rally and associate with people opposed to war? (In 1918, after

America had entered the war, Debs was arrested and given a ten-year prison sentence.) Compulsory military training was begun at Central High, with drills every week under a tough Army sergeant. Langston became a second lieutenant in the ROTC.

Working at a soda fountain on Central Avenue, in the heart of the Negro neighborhood, Langston dished up ice cream and watermelon and listened to the talk. He found some people were for the war, others against it. The women who supported it were busy sewing for the Red Cross or organizing Liberty Bond clubs. They believed—or maybe they just hoped—that the world would really become safe for democracy, even in America, when the war ended, and that black folks wouldn't be Jim Crowed any more.

The others complained about the high rents and the high prices and said bitterly that, no matter what the Negro did on the battlefield or on the home front, it wouldn't impress the white folks. They would act just as mean as they always had.

But not all of them were mean. There was Miss Clara Dieke, for instance, who taught painting and ceramics. In her mid-thirties then, she had studied abroad, and, to the small number of students interested, she brought the newest developments in art and teaching. The skills were hard to learn, but she made Langston see that you just had to get started on a picture or piece of pottery and stick with it till you finished it. You couldn't learn anything new or difficult if you didn't work hard at it.

Miss Helen M. Chesnutt, a graduate of Central's Class of 1897 and of Wellesley College, was another teacher who influenced Langston, although he never studied her subject, Latin. The only Negro teacher in the school, she was the daughter of Charles W. Chesnutt, the nationally known Cleveland lawyer-novelist. Both father and daughter could easily have passed as whites if they had chosen. Miss Chesnutt stood for the highest standards in scholarship. Even a mild compliment from her on one of his poems or stories appearing in the school magazine was a great reward for Langston. Because he liked her so much, he brought many other students into the Garden Club she sponsored. At its meetings she led the members into unsuspected scientific paths. Her annual home Christmas parties brought many club members into a world of quiet elegance they had never seen. Her own strength of character, and her indirect suggestions were important influences on Langston. (Only a few months before his death, in 1967, he sent the eighty-six-year-old retired teacher a book of poems and a letter signed "Affectionately, with happy memories, Langston.")

Most important of all, there was Miss Ethel Weimer, the school's most popular English teacher, daughter of a local high-school principal. About thirty then, she was one of those marvelous, lovely spinsters (women could not marry then and remain in the system) who chose their family from among their pupils. She opened Shakespeare's world to Langston when she read the plays aloud in her deep, dramatic voice. It was in her class that he discovered Carl Sandburg. Miss Weimer was not the kind of teacher who feared the new or the unpopular. And in the beginning, Sandburg was both. His first poems had been appearing in print for only a few years. His poem on Chicago, "hog butcher for the world," shocked and enraged many critics and teachers. No real poet, they said, chose such sordid subjects or used such brutal language.

But when Miss Weimer brought Sandburg's poems into the classroom, Langston found that this man said something direct and powerful, and said it about people Langston knew.

A bar of steel—it is only
Smoke at the heart of it, smoke and the blood
of a man.

Pittsburgh, Youngstown, Birmingham, Gary—Sandburg sang of the steel-making towns and the workers they killed. This was the Cleveland Langston knew, too, and his stepfather, Homer Clarke, was ground down by the chill blue steel. Sandburg, the Midwesterner, had dug deep into the new industrial America. He had been porter, truckman, dishwasher, harvest hand, construction worker, soldier, janitor, reporter. He knew the cities and their teeming streets and tenements, the cruel clash of men and machinery, the raw exploitation of the money-makers.

He knew it all, and he protested against what it was doing to men. In his poems were grief and sorrow. But in them too Langston heard the note of exultation. At the root of Sandburg's poetry was love of life, imagination that responded to tenderness and laughter, beauty and nature. He was raw and violent, true, but he was also delicate and lyrical.

It was not only what Sandburg wrote about, but how he wrote it, that excited Langston. Sandburg wrote free verse, that is, verse with an irregular rhythm, and usually without rhyme. And the language he used was often as simple as the common tongue, with the rhythms and bite and color that could lift the speech of ordinary folk into music. He used slang in his verses, and images that come out of the work men do.

Already Sandburg was being followed by other poets. One of them especially Langston was excited to come across. He was Fenton Johnson, a Chicagoan now, like Sandburg, but a Negro writer. Langston read his poems and recognized the despair they came out of: *I am tired of work; I am tired of building up somebody else's civilization . . . let the old shanty go to rot, the white people's clothes turn to dust . . . Throw the children into the river; civilization has given us too many. It is better to die than to grow up and find that you are colored.*

There were other new poets Miss Weimer introduced to him—Vachel Lindsay, Edgar Lee Masters,

Amy Lowell, Robert Frost. Reading poetry, he learned, was not just letting something happen to you; it was taking part in the poem's action. When it raised "that desirable gooseflesh" (in Emily Dickinson's words) he knew he was reading a true poem. These were the years when poets were beginning to explore new techniques. They broke free from the traditional patterns of poetry and with daring ingenuity tried to find their own voice and their own form. The new poets felt they could shape technique as they grew, making a form under the pressure of the experience created in the poem.

Miss Weimer, no writer herself, knew the art of encouraging creative expression in others. She gave her students a good deal of freedom in class and, when she saw Langston struggling to find his voice, she let him know her enthusiasm. She could make a student feel excited at having written something original, no matter how little a thing it was.

When Langston tried his hand, he was imitating, of course. But as the great French poet Paul Valéry said, "Nothing is more original, nothing truer to oneself, than to feed upon others' minds. Only be sure that you digest them. The lion consists of assimilated sheep."

Like all growing writers, Langston borrowed and echoed the work of those who were running before him. But he would soon begin to show his own originality and creativity.

Meanwhile, not all his learning was coming out of books. In his freshman year at Central he worked after school behind the soda fountain. When summer came, he had to find a full-time job. But war or no war, many employers would still not hire Negroes. Yes, they needed help, but they'd do anything rather than take on a Negro. "Pure" Americans— white, Anglo-Saxon Protestants—came first. After them the children of the foreign-born, even "kikes," "spicks," "hunkies." A colored boy came last of all.

Finally he got a job running a dumbwaiter in a big department store. It carried stock from the storeroom to the different departments. He saw that some people could pay fifty dollars for a bottle of perfume, or spend on a fancy cigarette case what was six months rent for his family.

The next summer he joined his mother in Chicago. (She and her husband were separated again.) As they rode up to her place on the streetcar, he wondered if this was the Chicago he had dreamed of back in Lawrence. Huge warehouses blackened with dirt lined the streets. Then he saw dull stretches of boxlike tenements. No yards, no trees, no grass. Bleak little stores edged the hot pavement. Negroes leaned out of windows or fanned themselves in doorways. When they reached his mother's home, they climbed the dark stairs and walked down a gloomy hallway smelling of hair oil and cabbage. At the rear end was their room, with two windows overlooking an alley.

Langston and his mother and brother sweated through the murderously hot summer months in that hole on Wabash Street. The elevated trains rushed past, shaking the house and thundering through the walls. Day and night the room was full of sounds of brawling in the street.

His mother had a job cooking for a lady who owned a fashionable hat shop, and Langston was taken on as a delivery boy. On his first Sunday off, he wandered outside the Negro neighborhood, exploring the city. A gang of white boys jumped him, yelling that they didn't allow niggers in their neighborhood. They knocked him down and beat him up. That night his jaw began to swell, but he was ashamed to tell his mother he had been licked in a fight. In the morning, when the swelling was bigger, his mother hustled him to a doctor. "Mumps!"

said the man, and prescribed the treatment. Langston never told him or his mother any better.

That summer the air seemed to smoke, Chicago was so hot. He went to the shore of Lake Michigan for relief, but the beach was like hot metal and the water was crowded with bathers, all of them black, for there were big stretches of water the Negroes couldn't swim in. These were for whites only, and it was risky to go there.

Fall came at last, and time for school to open. As often happened, whenever his "amiable but unpredictable" stepfather had wandered away, his mother urged him to stay on and keep working to help her out. He argued with her. What sense was there in quitting school for an unskilled job? Where would it get him? He had seen too many other of his friends give up school for little or nothing. No, he knew what he wanted and so his mother stayed on in Chicago, clinging to her job, while he went alone back to Cleveland. The little money he had managed to save he used to pay for a room. He couldn't afford to eat out, nor did he know how to cook, beyond boiling rice. So every night it was rice and hot dogs, hot dogs and rice. Then into bed to read and study until sleep came.

His reading ranged widely now, encouraged by

his teachers and by the local librarian, Effie Lee Power. For a time it would be a spurt of philosophy —Schopenhauer and Nietzsche. Then he would turn to novels, trying the popular Edna Ferber or the tougher Theodore Dreiser. From schoolmates he borrowed *The Gadfly,* Ethel Voynich's novel of Russians rebelling against the Tsar, and *Jean-Christophe,* Romain Rolland's huge story of the struggles of a young composer to find himself. With his high school French he tried to decipher Maupassant, and was elated one night to find the words, the phrases, whole paragraphs were suddenly flowing like his own language into his head. He could *read* French! And the beauty of the stories was *his.* No longer wrestling with dictionary and grammar, he could enjoy the realism and the psychological acuteness of the French writer. The fact that the people in the stories lived in a world and culture thousands of miles away did not make them remote or foreign. Maupassant knew how to connect their lives with his. The humanness of the characters reached out and touched him, lying alone here on his bed in a Cleveland rooming house. Maybe I can learn to write like this, he thought. There must be hundreds of stories about my own people, waiting to be told, stories people in far-off lands would read, even after I'm gone.

He didn't think he could write those stories now. Nothing like that took shape in the sixteen-year-old's mind. He did write one story, but only because it was a class assignment. It was a little thing, hardly two hundred words, about a white scrubwoman named Mary Winosky.

But poems—that was something else. It was almost as though he couldn't help himself. The lines came freely to him now no matter where he was or what he was doing. He could be on a streetcar and hear a line going through his head. He would fish in his pocket for a scrap of paper and write it down quickly, before it could disappear. Later he would copy it into a notebook.

Some of his writing appeared in "Belfry Owl," a department of Central's *Monthly*, which he edited and which Miss Weimer was advisor to. The Jelliffes remembered that his greatest pleasure came from his writing when he was growing up. "He glowed from it," they said. And the feeling lasted. Years later he told them, "I never quite escape the feeling of guilt about taking money for my poems. It doesn't seem decent to earn money from anything that you enjoy so much. Maybe I ought to make my living some other way."

Some of his poems he wasn't showing to anyone. They were too close to him. He couldn't risk being laughed at. It was safer, somehow, to test them on strangers who had never heard of Langston Hughes. He mailed a few to a magazine in New York. Back they came, with a printed slip that said, no, thanks. One magazine after another, and it was always the same. Once, however, the *Liberator*'s editor took the trouble to scrawl a friendly word across the rejection slip.

5 *Hurry Up!*
Hurry Up!

In his junior year at Central High, Langston didn't have to live alone for long, for his mother and stepfather got together again in Cleveland. His mother had found a job waiting on table in a Central Avenue restaurant. That November of 1918 the war ended in Europe, and the whole town came out on the streets to celebrate the Armistice. Negroes yelled and danced and waved flags like everybody else, for they were proud of the record black troops had made on the battlefields of Europe. They had suffered and died "to make the world safe for democracy" while their own freedom was still denied.

It didn't take long for the good feeling of celebration to wear off. Cleveland had been one of the more liberal towns for Negroes. But now the color line was drawn tighter and tighter. Landlords boosted rents sky-high at the sight of a dark skin. Theaters and hotels that had once accepted Negroes began barring them. And as white veterans applied for jobs, Negroes were often fired to make places for them.

One afternoon Langston's French class went downtown to see a matinee performance of the great French actress, Sarah Bernhardt. She was nearing the end of her life then, but her famous golden voice was still thrilling to hear. Afterward Langston and a white friend went across the street to eat in a big cafeteria with low prices that suited a schoolboy's pocket. They walked down the self-service line, the white boy in front, selecting their food, and stopped before the cashier's desk. She rang up the first boy's bill, and he paid her and went to find a table. She glanced up at Langston, then down at his tray. Furiously her fingers punched at the cash register. It rang and rang and rang till he thought it would never stop. Finally she yanked out the check and flung it on his tray. It read $8.65!

His friend's check had been only forty-five cents, and they had each taken about the same amount of food. Langston looked in amazement at the cashier.

"Why did *my* food cost so much?" he asked. "If you eat in here," she said, "that's the price you'll pay." "But I don't have that much food," he protested. Her face reddened, and she yelled, "Pay that check or put the tray down and get out!"

He put down his tray and walked over to where his friend was eating. Everyone was looking at them.

The white boy was astonished. He couldn't understand what had happened. He had never realized this went on in the democratic land his parents had come all the way across the sea to find. Langston was furious but he said nothing when his friend tried to patch up the humiliation with talk. They never went there again.

In the spring a letter came from his father in Mexico. It was a strange letter to get from a father who hadn't seen or written to his son for eleven years. Except for signing it "Affectionately," James N. Hughes wrote it as though he were giving an order to a servant. He would be in the States on business in June, he wrote, and "You are to accompany me to Mexico for the summer."

Langston and his mother took the news very differently. She was angered. It was just like that evil man, she said, to take her boy from her the moment he was big enough to help support the family. But Langston wanted to go. He couldn't help it: he wasn't leaving forever, just for the summer. His mother cried and cried but his stepfather said go ahead, it will be a good thing for you.

So he went, and discovered his father. He wasn't like the tall rider Langston had dreamed about. He was a little man, and wore a mustache. And he was cold. The minute they met he said mean things about Langston's mother, and never a word about being glad to see his son.

His father's headquarters were in Toluca, a town in a beautiful valley high up in the mountains. A snowcapped volcano looked down on the rambling, blue-white house. In the patio untended flowers and grass grew raggedly, for Mr. Hughes didn't care about anything that didn't pay. He was more concerned with the horses and chickens and cow in the corral at the back of the house. Maximiliano, the Indian boy who did the chores, was Langston's only friend. He slept on old sacks in the tool shed because Mr. Hughes didn't believe in giving Indians anything, even a bed. They wouldn't appreciate it, he said. When Langston learned his father paid the boy and the cook almost nothing, he gave them part of his allowance.

No one spoke English, which forced Langston to learn Spanish rapidly. Maximiliano taught him how to ride a horse without saddle or stirrups. There was nothing else to do in Toluca, except for a weekly movie. He didn't even visit his father's ranch because bandits were said to be around. Nor was he allowed to go into Mexico City.

When his father bothered to talk to him, it was to nag him about learning to do bookkeeping. Langston tried to please him, but he was always bad at figures and made a hopeless mess of them. "Seventeen and you can't add yet!" his father would yell at him.

The weeks droned by and Langston felt this was turning out to be the worst summer he had ever known. When he could admit it to himself, he knew he didn't like his father. What was there to like about a man who had his mind on just one thing—making money? Not that his mother and stepfather weren't interested in making money too. But money to them was for spending, to have a good time with. To his father, money was a means to make more money and still more money.

His father couldn't be blamed for hating the color line at home that kept Negroes from making a decent living. In the States he couldn't get into law school or professional associations. He couldn't get loans from banks, or insurance to protect his business. He couldn't live where he liked or go where he pleased. In Mexico these bars were down. Here he was able to practice law, buy property, lend money, own a ranch, handle mortgages. His own country did not allow a Negro to be a man; Mexico did. As James Hughes saw it, no self-respecting black would want to live out his life in a Jim Crow country. So, like many before him, he had gotten up and left.

The son couldn't quarrel with his father for that. But there was more to it. Something had gone wrong with his father. His natural rage at the injustice suffered by blacks had turned into contempt for the people who continued to live under it. The Negro who hid his real thoughts and feelings, who did not openly criticize and complain, whose honesty and openness gave way to patience and submission, he despised. He made no effort to understand or to change others. He only hated. James Hughes himself became the only object of his concern. He had no use for poor people: it was their own fault they were poor. As for Mexicans, he said they were lazy, ignorant, backward. They were just like the Negroes back home.

Langston saw his father had come to hate not the oppressors, but the oppressed, not the murderer, but the victim. And his hatred included himself, for being black. Flight was his only solution. Again and again he pounded at Langston: don't stay in the United States when you finish high school. Leave it, and never go back. If you stay there, he warned, you will only be a barber or a bellhop all your life.

He rarely talked of anything else. He had no time for it. He drove himself relentlessly from dawn to almost midnight. He was always yelling "Hurry up! Hurry up!" at Langston. No one worked fast enough for him.

Shut out from his father's life, Langston found he had nothing to say to him. He stopped trying, and fell silent. The summer passed without a word from his mother in Cleveland. He understood her better now. No wonder she could not live with his father. But why had they married in the first place? And why had they had him? Once, sunk into deep misery, he took a loaded pistol from his father's desk and held it for a long time to his head. But his natural zest for life took over. There were dozens of things he wanted to see and do, and would pulling the trigger make him happier? He put the pistol back in the desk.

The blues persisted, and at last even his father took notice. He offered to take Langston to Mexico City for the bullfights. When the morning to depart came they rose very early to catch the first train. "Hurry up and get dressed!" his father yelled through the dark. When they sat down to breakfast, his father gulped the food down and then for no reason at all barked out another "Hurry up!"

Langston's stomach churned. He couldn't swallow. His eyes burned. He trembled violently. He clenched his fist to smash his father in the face. But instead he rose and went back to bed, the room whirling and his mouth filled with a vile taste.

His father shrugged and went off without him. For four days Maximiliano and the cook tended Langston, puzzled by his strange condition. Then his father came back and, finding his son still in bed and burning with fever, sent for a doctor. He was taken to a hospital in Mexico City, where examinations showed nothing. But still his eyes had turned a deep yellow and he was very sick. No one could understand what was wrong with him.

He never told anyone he was sick because he hated his father.

In September he started back to school in Cleveland. The only way he could get sleeping-car space after crossing the border into Texas was to pretend to be Mexican. He passed the ticket window marked COLORED, went into the white waiting room, asked in Spanish for a berth, and got it with no trouble. When he had to change trains in St. Louis, he asked for a soda at the refreshment counter. The soda jerk asked him whether he was Mexican or Negro. Feeling he was now in the free North, Langston replied, "Negro." The man turned away to serve someone else.

Now he knew he was home.

6   *I've Known Rivers*

    Unhappy as that summer of 1919 had been for him, Langston returned from Mexico to find it had been unqualified hell for the people back home. The "Red Summer," they called it, red for the blood that flowed. The black troops arriving home from Europe had been greeted by hurrahs that faded fast. Within months ten Negro veterans still in uniform were lynched by mobs. In Chicago, a race riot had raged through the city for thirteen days, with twenty-three Negroes and fifteen whites dead at the end, and over five hundred people injured. Negroes had fought for democracy abroad and were ready to die for it at home. The terror had gone on all summer and would not let up. By the year's end riots had burned and ravaged twenty-five cities.

In the *Liberator,* Langston read Claude McKay's shout of defiance:

If we must die—let it not be like hogs,
Hunted and penned in an inglorious spot . . .
Like men we'll face the murderous, cowardly pack
Pressed to the wall, dying, but fighting back!

Langston was back in school for his senior year. With horror almost daily in the headlines, the classroom seemed as remote from reality as another planet. He was elected editor of the yearbook, and class poet—this time an honor he had really earned by his poems published in the school magazine. One of them was his tribute to Carl Sandburg:

Carl Sandburg's poems
Fall on the white pages of his books
Like blood-clots of song
From the wounds of humanity.
I know a lover of life sings
When Carl Sandburg sings.
I know a lover of all the living
Sings then.

Many more poems went into his notebook, where he carefully kept trifles apart from the verses he felt were true poems. One of these came out of a gym dance where his eye had fallen on a slim, chocolate-brown girl in a red dress. She was seventeen, his own age, and had just moved up from the South. For her he wrote this poem:

When Susanna Jones wears red
Her face is like an ancient cameo
Turned brown by the ages.

Come with a blast of trumpets,
Jesus!

When Susanna Jones wears red
A queen from some time-dead Egyptian night
Walks once again.

Blow trumpets, Jesus!

And the beauty of Susanna Jones in red
Burns in my heart a love-fire sharp like pain.

Sweet silver trumpets,
Jesus!

As graduation came near, he began to worry about what was coming after. His classwork had been very good except for math and chemistry. The only course he barely squeaked through was public speaking, although he would spend a sizable part of his adult life earning money on the platform. His over-all average was 87.3 per cent. Central had prepared students well for college, but few, especially the ten Negroes in the class, expected to go. Most families, like Langston's, could not afford it. Then word came from his father in Mexico. There was a hint in the letter that if Langston visited him again the coming summer, he might send him to college.

Again his mother tried to keep him in Cleveland. She wanted Langston to get a job now to help her out. After last summer's misery, he didn't want to go to Mexico either. But what would happen if he didn't? Would he ever get a better education? And how much real help would he be to his mother if he was never trained for anything better than being a porter or a busboy?

It was a good argument, but his mother disliked his father so much she wouldn't listen. Langston began to feel that the sooner he was on his own altogether, the better. Even though the road to independence might take him through Mexico, where his father was, he had to follow it.

He took the train, feeling blue. He was leaving behind a city and a life he knew, and stepping off into the dark. Perhaps he sensed that from now on he was going to have to make it on his own. He did not know how he would do it, or whether he could. He did not know what he would be, what he could make of himself. He could not look to his mother for help. She was so weighed down by the struggle to survive she could think of little beyond the next week's pay. His father he hated, and yet he had to rely on him.

His blues were to last a long time—for the next three or four years, he said later. And yet those were the years when he wrote a great many poems, and some of his best. It was usually when he was unhappy that he wrote. It built a pressure inside him that he could relieve only by shaping his feelings into poetry. His poems were like the blues, "songs folks make up when their heart hurts."

On the train that first day, heading south for Mexico, he wrote the lines that became one of his best-known poems. Here in his own words is the story of how he made it:

All day on the train I had been thinking about my father and his strange dislike of his own people. I didn't understand it, because I was a Negro, and I liked Negroes very much. . . . I never tired of hearing them talk, listening to the thunderclaps of their laughter, to their troubles, to their discussions. . . . They seemed to me like the gayest and the bravest people possible . . . facing tremendous odds, working and laughing and trying to get somewhere in the world. . . . It was just sunset, and we crossed the Mississippi, slowly, over a long bridge. I looked out the window of the Pullman at the great muddy river flowing down toward the heart of the South, and I began to think what that river, the old Mississippi, had meant to Negroes in the past . . . how Abraham Lincoln had made a trip down the Mississippi on a raft to New Orleans, and how he had seen slavery at its worst, and had decided within himself that it should be removed from American life. Then I began to think about other rivers in our past—the Congo, and the Niger, and the Nile in Africa—and the thought came to me: "I've known rivers," and I put it down on the back of an envelope I had in my pocket, and within the space of ten or fifteen minutes, as the train gathered speed in the dusk, I had written this poem. . . .

He called it "The Negro Speaks of Rivers." He was eighteen when he wrote it, and it remained one of his favorite poems all his life:

I've known rivers:
I've known rivers ancient as the world and older
than the flow of human blood in human veins.

My soul has grown deep like the rivers.

I bathed in the Euphrates when dawns were young.
I built my hut near the Congo and it lulled me to
sleep.
I looked upon the Nile and raised the pyramids
above it.
I heard the singing of the Mississippi when Abe
Lincoln went down to New Orleans and I've seen
its muddy bosom turn all golden in the sunset.
I've known rivers:
Ancient, dusky rivers.

My soul has grown deep like the rivers.

This is the poem as everyone knows it now. It began inside him with a feeling or mood that drew in what he was looking at, memories of what he had done or read, and condensed them into the first lines. Then the rest flowed out quickly, often to remain the way it came, except for a word changed here and there or a line crossed out.

Exactly how a poem gets written even the writer himself has great trouble explaining. Laurence Sterne once said, "I begin with the first sentence, trusting to Almighty God for the second." Langston would have added, put it down fast when it comes, "for poems are like rainbows: they escape you quickly."

The beautiful "Rivers" poem reveals some significant things. Feeling himself one with all blacks, Langston used the world "soul" in the refrain, and was perhaps one of the first to give it the same meaning it would come to have almost fifty years later for all young blacks. (His use probably goes back to Du Bois's *The Souls of Black Folk,* the book that was his Bible in boyhood. And it is worth noting that he dedicated this poem to Dr. Du Bois.) He had used the words earlier, in his "Song of the Soul of Central," a long poem in free verse published in *The Monthly* in January 1919. There he spoke of the School's soul being always "young," "beautiful," and "great" because it knew no race or creed and taught all students to be brothers. The other interesting point is his identification with Africa as the homeland of his ancestors.

That summer in Toluca wasn't quite as bad as he had feared—perhaps because his father was away at the ranch so much. The small town was a lonely place for a boy. He missed having Negro friends to hang around with. He read a lot, improving his Spanish on novels, and rode his horse.

Mexican revolutionaries were all over the countryside, organizing the peons against the landlords and fighting the government's army. The Zapatistas (as they were called after their leader, Emiliano Zapata) had taken all the cattle and sheep from his father's ranch. Bandits, his father said bitterly, out for nothing but to destroy property. When Langston said he had heard they only wanted to get the land back for the peons, his father cried, "Lies! All lies!"

Talk about college plans was put off again and again. Then one afternoon, when they were riding together, his father announced he had decided Langston should become a mining engineer. There would be plenty of work for him at the mines near the ranch. Langston protested. He was no good at math. Nonsense, his father said. If you want to learn, you can. Engineers make money. Don't you want to get anywhere? Yes, said Langston, but I want to be a *writer.*

That began a quarrel. Langston insisted he wanted only to write, and his father replied that writers didn't make money, and certainly not colored writers. To James Hughes the only thing for a sensible Negro to do was to master something that would enable him to make a living anywhere in the world, and then get out of the States. Don't stay home, he said, "where you have to live like a nigger with niggers." When Langston said he liked his own people, and had lots of fun with them, his father exploded. How can anybody have fun living behind the color line? he yelled.

The argument went on and on. You must go to a college in Europe, his father said. Langston suggested Columbia instead, mainly because it was in New York and he had an aching desire to see Harlem. Europe, New York; New York, Europe —they fought for the rest of the summer. September came and his father wouldn't give in. Not a penny would he spend on educating his son in the country he hated.

Langston decided he'd better earn money of his

own, and find some means of getting away from his father. He began teaching English in a private business school and in a girls' finishing school. He used the Berlitz method, instructing only in English. It worked, and his pupils learned. He stayed on all winter, and now that he had his own money to spend, went up to Mexico City on weekends for the bullfights.

He began to try to write prose, little pieces about Toluca, and then a short play for children. The natural place to send his work was a new magazine for children started by Dr. Du Bois and the *Crisis* staff. *The Brownie's Book* began publishing his sketches and poems in January 1921 and sent him warm letters. Encouraged, he mailed in the poem he had written on the train. Then, almost leaping out of page 71 in the June issue of *The Crisis,* he saw "A Negro Speaks of Rivers." Below it was the name, LANGSTON HUGHES. He looked at it so often he must have read the ink off the page. It was his first poem to appear in a magazine for adults.

In July *The Crisis* carried his poem about his grandmother, "Aunt Sue's Stories," and then letters, essays and more poems. Langston's father was impressed, at first, but not after he learned his poet son earned nothing for this work. It didn't matter to Langston. He was in print, and he knew that others were reading him.

Perhaps because he, too, secretly enjoyed seeing the family name in print, Mr. Hughes yielded at last, and offered to put Langston through Columbia. Langston applied, and was admitted. He kept teaching through the summer, turning over his class in the final days to a white woman from Arkansas, who told him in amazement that she had "never come across an educated Nigra before."

He left Toluca in the early fall, glad to go. The train took him to Vera Cruz for the boat to New York. There, at the Gulf of Mexico, he saw the ocean for the first time. And then at last the sunlit towers of Manhattan rising out of the green sea.

7 *Columbia vs. Harlem*

Heading for Harlem he took his first subway ride. The train rushed madly through the tunnel, green lights punctuating the dark and stations suddenly glaring whitely and then blacking out. He counted off the numbered signs till 135th Street and got off. The platform was jammed with people—colored people—on their way to work. Lugging his heavy bags up the steps, he came out breathless on the corner of Lenox Avenue. The September morning was clear and bright. He stood there, feeling good. It was a crazy feeling—as though he had been homesick for this place he'd never been to.

He walked down the block to register at the YMCA, the first place young Negroes stayed when they hit Harlem. That afternoon he crossed the street to visit the Harlem Branch Library. All newcomers were swiftly made at home there by Miss Ernestine Rose, the white librarian, and her *café-au-lait* assistant, Catherine Latimer, who had charge of the Schomburg Collection. Here you could drown in thousands and thousands of books by and about black folks. That night, dazzled by the electric signs on the marquee, he went into the Lincoln Theatre to hear a blues singer.

He had a week to himself before classes began at Columbia, and he spent every moment mapping Harlem with his feet. The great dark expanse of this island within an island fascinated him. In 1921 it ran from 127th Street north to 145th, and from Madison Avenue west to Eighth Avenue. Eighty thousand black people (it would be three times that number within ten years) were packed into the long rows of once private homes as the flood of Southern Negroes continued to roll North. It was a new black colony in the midst of the Empire City, the biggest of the many "Bronzevilles" and "Black Bottoms" beginning to appear across the nation.

The high rents charged Negroes and the low wages paid them made Harlem a profitable colony for landlords and merchants, but a swollen, aching slum for the people who lived there. To the boy from the Midwest, however, this was not yet its meaning. He had been in love with Harlem long before he got there, and his dream was to become its poet. That first week of wonderful new insights and sounds passed swiftly. He loved the variety of faces —black, brown, peach, and beige—the richest range of types any place on earth. He hated to move out of Harlem, but his tuition was paid at Columbia and he felt he had to go. At the dormitory office they looked startled when he showed up for his room key. There must be some mistake, they told him; no room was left. He did not know it but Columbia did not allow Negroes to live in the dormitories. There was a big flurry when he insisted he had made a reservation long ago, by mail. He got the room finally, but it was a token of what was to come.

The university was too big, too cold. It was like being in a factory. Physics, math, French—he had trouble with all of them and the instructors were too busy or too indifferent to help. His only friend was Chun, a Chinese boy who didn't like Columbia either. Nobody asked the yellow man or the black man to join a fraternity and none of the girls would dance with them. Not being used to this, Chun expected them to. Langston didn't.

Nothing went right at school. Langston stopped studying, spent very little time on campus and all the time he could in Harlem or downtown. He made the city his school, read a lot of books, and dented his allowance badly buying tickets night after night for the all-Negro musical hit *Shuffle Along,* whose songs were written by Noble Sissle and Eubie Blake. His mother, separated again from Homer Clarke, showed up in New York and he had to help her with money while she looked for work.

All the time, feeling out of place at Columbia, he kept writing poems. That winter he sent several to *The Crisis,* and in January his "Negro" appeared, with these lines, which open and close the poem:

> I am a Negro:
> Black as the night is black,
> Black like the depths of my Africa.

The editors of *The Crisis* awoke to the fact that the boy who had been sending them poems from Toluca was now in New York. They invited him to lunch. Langston panicked, imagining they were all so rich or remote that he wouldn't know what to say. Much as he admired Dr. Du Bois, he was afraid to show the great man how dumb he was. He went, anyhow, taking along his mother for anchorage. Although they tried to put him at ease, telling him how much the readers liked his work, he was too scared to see any more of them.

Despite the little amount of time he said he spent on the campus, he did not do badly at Columbia. His final grades show three Bs, a C, and a failing F in physical education. He was given no grade at all in mathematics because he was absent so often. He had made no honors, but he didn't care, perhaps because it was honor enough to see his poems printed in *The Crisis* month after month. One of the staff even arranged for him to read his poems at the Community Church. These were signs that he was not standing still. But neither was he moving in the direction his father wanted him to go. So he wrote and said he was quitting college and going to work. He wouldn't ask for money any more.

His father never answered.

Langston was on his own. His mother had gone back to Cleveland. He took a room by himself in Harlem, and began to hunt for a job. It was June 1922, and business was booming. At least it looked like it from the number of help-wanted ads in the papers. Langston wasn't trained for much, so he followed up the unskilled jobs. But no matter what he applied for—office boy, busboy, clerk, waiter—the employer would always say he wasn't looking for a colored boy.

He turned to the employment agencies. It was no use here, either. Where was the job for a black man who wanted to work? Everyone was trying to prove Langston's father was right: the color line wouldn't let you live.

At last a Greek family gave him a job on their truck-garden farm on Staten Island. Color didn't matter to them if you were willing to work from dawn to dark for fifty dollars a month plus bed and board, with Sunday afternoons off.

It was hard work, but it felt good being out of doors and knowing you were helping to feed people. When the farming season ended he had enough money to buy an overcoat and rent a room in Harlem again. A job delivering flowers turned up; he couldn't stick at it because the boss was too much in a hurry, just like his father. He checked the want ads and the job agencies again, offered to shine shoes, run errands, wash dishes. No one wanted him.

He caught a whiff of sea air off the harbor one day and thought, why not try for a job aboard ship, and see the world? He walked the waterfront for weeks, till someone signed him on as a mess boy.

It turned out to be a big joke on himself. The rusty old freighter was going no further than Jones Point, a few hours up the Hudson, where it anchored next to scores of other empty government ships left over from the war.

Langston's was a mother ship, manned by a small crew whose job it was to keep the machinery oiled and the cables in place on board about twenty other ships. Dead ships, and a dead winter, going nowhere. The nearest place ashore was nothing but a whistlestop for trains.

He was the only Negro among the crew. After work, they passed the time sleeping, playing cards, or talking. He liked listening to the sailors, their bragging about the foreign ports they'd seen, the women they'd loved, the fighting they'd been in.

Alone in the long cold nights with snow blanketing the river and the ships creaking in the wind he would get close to the radiator and work his way through the ship's library. He found Samuel Butler's great novel about a boy growing up and his fights

with his father, *The Way of All Flesh,* and Joseph
Conrad's novel of the Congo, *Heart of Darkness.*

It might have been a wasted winter, but for one
thing. He wrote a poem called "The Weary Blues."
It was one of the earliest folk portraits he would do,
this time of a Harlem man he had heard playing the
piano and singing:

Droning a drowsy syncopated tune,
Rocking back and forth to a mellow croon,
    I heard a Negro play.
Down in Lenox Avenue the other night
By the pale dull pallor of an old gas light
    He did a lazy sway . . . .
    He did a lazy sway . . . .
To the tune o' those Weary Blues.
With his ebony hands on each ivory key
He made that poor piano moan with melody.
    O Blues!
Swaying to and fro on his rickety stool
He played that sad raggy tune like a musical fool.
    Sweet Blues!
Coming from a black man's soul.
    O Blues!
In a deep song voice with a melancholy tone

I heard that Negro sing, that old piano moan—
    "Ain't got nobody in all this world,
      Ain't got nobody but ma self.
      I's gwine to quit ma frownin'
      And put ma troubles on the shelf."
Thump, thump, thump, went his foot on the floor.
He played a few chords then he sang some more—
    "I got the Weary Blues
      And I can't be satisfied.
      Got the Weary Blues
      And can't be satisfied—
      I ain't happy no mo'
      And I wish that I had died."
And far into the night he crooned that tune.
The stars went out and so did the moon.
The singer stopped playing and went to bed.
While the Weary Blues echoed through his head
He slept like a rock or a man that's dead.

Somehow he had trouble making the poem come out right. He worked at it all winter, trying one ending after another. Later, when he was satisfied, he sent it off to the *Amsterdam News,* a Harlem paper, where it appeared on April 8, 1923.

"The Weary Blues" catches the essence of that

left-lonesome mood, although it does not use the blues form itself, except for the quoted lines within the poem. Its subtly syncopated rhythm shows an innate musical sense. The poem is jazz in words, the heartache music he heard coming out of the people he grew up with.

"The Weary Blues" is also a sign of how far young Langston had gone along the road mapped out by Sandburg and the other new poets. He was neither sentimental nor preachy. He displayed no false optimism and sought no romantic escape. The speech he used was not stiff and artificial but natural and human. Instead of pleading their case, he tried to express his people's inmost feelings.

In the spring, the riverbanks fuzzed green and ships began moving up and down. This was no time for him to be sitting. He quit the mothballed fleet, getting an excellent reference from the steward. It worked at the first shipping office he visited. He was placed as a steward on the S.S. *Malone,* a freighter bound for Africa.

He brought with him a box of books he had stored in Harlem over the winter. Off Sandy Hook that first night out he opened the box and looked over the books. Then he suddenly grabbed one after the other and hurled them over the rail far out into the sea. It was as though he were tossing away his past, the lonely years of wandering from town to town, attic to basement, from mother who left him to father he couldn't love. It was everything he hoped to get rid of. Going out to Africa was leaping the barriers of race and fear of poverty. He was twenty-one now, a man, and on his own. "I felt that nothing would ever happen to me again that I didn't want to happen."

Four bells sounded. He tossed the last book out and lost sight of it as it went down in the dark.

Then he went to bed.

8   *Africa*

The first day out the sailors were busy polishing
the brass, chipping the decks and painting the bulk-
heads. The freighter was loaded with machinery,
tools and canned goods, and carried six passengers,
all of them missionaries. There were forty-two men
in the crew. Langston bunked with the two other
mess boys—George, a Kentucky Negro, and Ramón,
a chocolate-colored Puerto Rican.

The job was not hard. He took care of the petty
officers' mess and made up their staterooms. There
were many free hours to lie around in the June sun,
play cards, or just sleep. It felt good to know that
the six months ahead would be free of worry about
finding a job or going hungry or being homeless.

The S.S. *Malone* stopped briefly at the Azores and
the Canaries. Langston was impatient: he couldn't

wait to see Africa. At last they sighted the coast through the haze of light. The ship pulled in closer and the green hills stood up, the sandy beach gleaming below them, and palm trees soaring to the sky.

They docked at Dakar, and he couldn't believe he was really here, in Africa. In his mind at that time there must have been a confusing blur of impressions. In school the geographies painted Africa a dark jungle land full of primitive peoples. The histories ignored it, as though nothing worthwhile had ever been shaped there. Slavery was always linked to Africa, and the movies showed Africans as half-naked savages with spears.

But challenging the old image of Africa was the steady force of Du Bois's writing on African culture in *The Crisis*. At the Schomburg Collection Langston had seen for himself the African sculptures and masks, and the books of the many explorers and travelers and scholars who told of Africa's true life and history. Coming to New York at the peak of Marcus Garvey's "Back to Africa" movement, he had seen thousands of Harlemites responding to the black Jamaican's appeal to break out from the despair of the ghetto and the ring of hostile whites. Be proud of your past, Garvey kept saying, proud of the great empires built by black men in Africa's glorious age. Blackness is not a badge of inferiority, he said; blackness is beauty and strength. And Africa is the homeland of all the black peoples of the world. We must retake it from the white men who rule it and make it a black republic where we shall all be free and equal.

And now Langston was here, in the homeland of his imaginings. In the ports African stevedores unloaded the *Malone*'s cargo and carried aboard palm oil and cocoa beans and mahogany—American-made goods exchanged for the treasures taken out of the African earth. He found how little the traders and the shipowners paid for the riches they bought and the labor they hired. He saw the white man take what he wanted and do what he liked. The Africans lived under white laws made abroad for the black colonies, laws enforced by whip and gun. What about Garvey, they asked Langston, will he help free Africa and bring it unity? They wanted the white man to get off their backs and go away.

Feeling he shared and understood their burden, Langston told the Africans that as a black man his problems in America were something like theirs. But to his amazement they only looked at him and laughed. With his copper skin and straight black hair he was a white man to them, not a black. When he protested he was not white, they said he wasn't black either. People of mixed blood, like Langston, were "colored" to them, not black. And most of the colored foreigners who had come to Africa were either missionaries or colonial administrators, trying to tell them they had something better to offer Africa and nothing to learn from her. But Africans knew these people had come only to carry out the white man's desires. And in the Africans' eyes that made them all *white* men.

It hurt to be told he was not one of them. This color business was strange and paradoxical. At home, a dark skin automatically meant the denial of opportunity. And the darker the skin the darker your future. The color prejudice of the whites had even spread to many Negroes, who drew color lines within the color line. Most dark-skinned Negroes at that time did not like to be called black. They would rather be called brown-skinned. People of lighter color looked down on those of darker color, and the darker were often jealous and resentful of the lighter.

In one river port Langston got to know a sixteen-year-old mulatto boy, the son of an African mother and an English father, who had left them behind when he went home. The boy was terribly lonely because the English colony shunned him and would not give him work, while the Africans would not become his friends because his mother had chosen to live with a white man. Langston himself had many racial strains in his family, and this encounter struck home. Later he wrote of it in the short story "African Morning," and in the poem "Cross":

> My old man's a white old man
> And my old mother's black.
> If ever I cursed my white old man
> I take my curses back.
>
> If ever I cursed my black old mother
> And wished she were in hell,
> I'm sorry for that evil wish
> And now I wish her well.
>
> My old man died in a fine big house.
> My ma died in a shack.
> I wonder where I'm gonna die,
> Being neither white nor black?

He returned to the theme again and again in other stories and poems, and in his play *Mulatto*.

The *Malone* moved down the western shore of Africa, stopping at dozens of ports. Langston saw the Ivory Coast, the Gold Coast, and the Slave Coast, the Niger and the Congo, the Bight of Benin, Calabar and the Cameroons. He sent off to *The Crisis* an essay on his random impressions of "Ships, Sea and Africa." By the time the ship crossed the equator the crew's discipline had melted away. Their money went on liquor and girls. In port they were often drunk and quarrelsome, and sometimes aboard ship the captain could get work out of them only at the point of a gun.

It was a tough crew, but Langston got along well with everyone except the third engineer, a sour Southerner who talked loudly about "spicks" and "niggers." Once he started a row when Langston was feeding several Negro harbor officials, as was the custom, in his mess. When the engineer ordered them out Langston exploded and threatened him with the handiest weapon, a big metal soup tureen. The engineer fled, and left the Africans to finish their meal. He never bothered Langston again.

One night, walking in the streets of Burutu, a town on the Nigerian delta, Langston was invited into the house of Nagary, an old Mohammedan trader. As the moonlight flowed through the door and a big green parrot swayed on a ring hung from the roof, the trader opened his heavy boxes and showed Langston his goods. There was beaten brass from the Niger, beautifully carved little statues, brilliant cloth woven by women, the skins of jungle animals, and the soft feathers of birds whose flight had once lit up dark forests. One box was a treasure chest of ivories—great bracelets, milk-white ivory tusks, some carved with monkeys and coiled snakes, and tiny panels with dancing figures.

Nagary never asked him to buy. Langston's wonder and delight seemed enough for him. When he left, Nagary gave him a great spray of feathers and said, "God be with you." Down at the dock, Langston climbed the rope ladder to the deck and took a last look at the golden moon hanging like ripe fruit over Burutu.

He lay down on his bunk. They would soon be headed home again. He thought about the months in Africa, images mixed and clashing in his memory —the stunning beauty of the landscape, and black bodies swollen with elephantiasis, whites with guns in their belts ordering blacks about, missionary churches with Negroes segregated in the back pews, the clean beaches and the filthy freighters. It was a long time before he fell asleep.

Sailing home, they ran into a terrific hurricane in mid-ocean. Hundred-ton waves smashed over the deck, pounding two of their lifeboats to pieces. No one would go up on deck, for the wind could snatch a man and hurl him overboard.

The storm delayed them several days and the food ran low. The crew grumbled and swore, forgetting they had often stolen food from the storeroom to trade ashore for whiskey and women. They got down to eating musty old oatmeal crawling with tiny worms. Just before they reached the Virgin Islands the last dinner was a stew made up of scraps of garbage. If they had not made port the next day there would have been a riot aboard.

The *Malone* tied up at New York on a bright autumn day. Every member of the crew was paid off and fired. The men grabbed their money and raced ashore. Langston never saw any of them again.

9

A Garret
in Paris

With the money left over from his freighter pay, Langston bought a new suit and coat in New York and headed for home. "Home" was wherever his mother happened to be. This time she was living with his stepfather and brother in McKeesport, Pennsylvania. He brought them African souvenirs —hammered brass trays, beads, and rhinoceros-hide slippers. He stayed a few weeks and then came back to New York to look for another ship.

He got a berth as mess boy on a big freighter running between New York and Holland. The seas were mountain-high in the winter months. When they got to Rotterdam the second time he had had enough of howling storms. He drew the money due him and took the train for Paris. It was an early

February morning when he got off the train at the Gare du Nord. He had just turned twenty-two, he was in the Paris every young poet dreamed about, and he had seven dollars in his pocket.

He checked his bags and set out for a quick look at Paris. He could read the French signs and took a bus headed toward the center of the city. Getting out at the opera house, he walked along the broad boulevards in the snow, finally taking the bank of the Seine and ending up at the Louvre. It was warm in the vast museum. He looked at the paintings and statues until he felt tired and hungry.

Wandering the streets again, lonely and lost, he came across some Negro musicians at a little cafe. He hoped they could tell him where to find a cheap place to stay and a job. But they said he was crazy to think an unskilled foreigner—who couldn't even speak French—could land work when so many Frenchmen were jobless. He tried places where the people spoke English—the American Embassy and the American Library, the American Express and the Paris *Herald*. No job.

Meanwhile he had found a cheap little room in Montmartre and was living on nothing but coffee and one roll a meal. He liked Paris, but how could he go on? He was hungry all the time and growing desperate. He wrote his mother in McKeesport for a twenty-dollar loan. A long long month passed before a reply came. There was no money in the envelope, only a long list of her own troubles. She too had no money. His stepfather was very sick with pneumonia. His kid brother had been kicked out of school for fighting. And what are you doing bumming around in Paris (he could hear her angry voice rising) when we need you here at home?

He felt terrible, reading that, but how could he get home without any money? Then his luck changed and a Negro woman from Martinique hired him as doorman for her tiny nightclub in Montmartre. He bought a secondhand blue cap with some gold braid to look official. His pay in francs amounted to less than a quarter a night, with one meal thrown in. But there wasn't much choice. He picked up some tips running to the corner for cigarettes. He was supposed to be bouncer as well as doorman, but the brawls were too frequent and too bloody for him to do much.

A new friend came to the rescue. Rayford Logan, a Negro army officer who had stayed on in France for a while after the war, had read Langston's poems in *The Crisis* and looked him up. He helped Langston find a job as second cook in a nightclub. Not that he could cook, but it turned out they really wanted a dishwasher, so it didn't matter. His pay would be about seventy-five cents a night, and breakfast.

He was coming up in the world—from doorman to dishwasher. He liked working at the Grand Duc, which, in spite of its name, was only a little room with some small tables packed close, a bar, and space for barely a dozen couples to dance. Bruce, the cook, was big, brown-skinned, and one-eyed. But that one eye was fierce enough. Langston liked him because he wouldn't let anyone order him around, and he cooked a fried chicken you couldn't find anywhere else in Paris.

The best hours began around three in the morning, when, after the other clubs were closed, the musicians and entertainers would drop in at the Grand Duc and stay till seven or eight. New dances had just been brought over to Paris by Negro dancers from the States and everyone was doing them at the Grand Duc. They played and danced while he listened from the tiny kitchen, washing the last pots and pans. Back in his room in the tall old house near the Place Clichy, under a roof that slanted up to the eaves, he sat at the window overlooking the chimney pots of Paris and tried to get the same beat on paper, struggling to fit the rhythms of jazz into the rhythm of words:

> "Me an' ma baby's
> Got two mo' ways,
> Two mo' ways to do de buck!"
>   Da, da,
>   Da, da, da!
> Soft light on the tables,
> Music gay,
> Brown skin steppers
> In a cabaret.
>
> White folks, laugh!
> White folks, pray!
>
> "Me an' ma baby's
> Got two mo' ways,
> Two mo' ways to do de buck!"

(Later, when the Charleston came in, he changed "buck" to "Charleston" to modernize the poem.)

He mailed his poems to New York and magazines began to take them. *Vanity Fair* sent him $24.50 for three poems. It was the first time he had ever been paid for his writing.

Life wasn't all work that year. He had two love affairs in Paris. The first, with a Russian dancer, lasted a few months until Sonia had to go out of town for a job. The second was with a girl Rayford Logan introduced him to. Mary was a soft doeskin brown, the daughter of an African businessman from Lagos, and a white Englishwoman. Mary had been educated in London. She had read Langston's poems in *The Crisis.* He was a handsome young poet, hard for a girl to resist. They often went dancing at the Moulin Rouge or walking in the forest at Versailles. Soon they were falling in love, and Mary began to talk of eloping. But Langston couldn't see marriage when he didn't even have the price of a ring or a decent suit to get married in. Mary's father interfered as soon as he heard of the affair, and ordered her back to London at once. Their goodbye was sad but after a while Langston found the memory didn't hurt so much.

Just after the Grand Duc promoted him to waiter, business began to fall off. Langston decided to save some emergency money. He took to sleeping all day long to keep from eating any meals except at the club. One morning, wakened by a knock at the door, he opened it to find a small dapper man, wearing spats and carrying a cane. It was Dr. Alain Locke, professor of philosophy at Howard University in Washington. He knew Langston's poems and had tracked him through *The Crisis*. He took him to lunch and told him about a special Negro issue he was putting together for the magazine *Survey Graphic*.

Here was the first meeting of two of the most important figures in a movement just coming to birth—the Black Renaissance. Alain Locke was its midwife, the critic who would help young writers and artists find patrons and publication. And Langston Hughes would become the most creative and prolific writer produced by that movement.

Locke believed a new Negro was being shaped by the life of the black masses in the great cities. Their habits of life and their ways of thought were changing with incredible speed. Gone were the days of "Auntie" and "Mammy," of "Uncle Tom" and "Sambo." The new generation in the black ghettoes saw the great gap between America's democratic promises and its practice. A sense of community and racial solidarity was taking hold. Pride in race, pride in its past and its traditions, militancy in demanding full citizenship rights—the standards Du Bois had raised long ago—these were the mark of the new Negro. And black artists and writers were examining Negro life and history for themes that would enrich black culture.

It was a time for self-discovery, a time that coincided with Langston's own exploration of his inner resources and talents.

Dr. Locke asked Langston to go over with him those of his poems that might fit into the "new Negro" anthology. Locke chose eleven, many of them poems published that year in *The Crisis* or *Opportunity,* poems that would become his best-known—"Youth," "Dream Variation," "Minstrel Man," "Our Land," "I, Too, Sing America," "Jazzonia."

Later he took Langston to the Opéra and then arranged for him to see a superb private collection of African sculpture from Benin, the Sudan, and the Congo.

It was an exciting break in a summer that was going badly. Business was now so poor that the

Grand Duc decided to close down until the fall. Romeo, the other waiter, a friendly Italian of about Langston's age, asked him to come home with him on vacation. Langston had wanted to see Italy, and the fare was cheap, so he accepted. It was a wonderful week he had at Desenzano, Romeo's home town on the shore of Lake Garda in northern Italy. Above the old fishing port rose flowering fields and then the mountains. A great fuss was made over the visitor because he was the first Negro the townsfolk had ever seen. Everyone wanted to get a good look at him, touch him, and treat him to a glass of wine. Their curiosity was kindly and he enjoyed with them the village dances and the picnics in the ancient olive groves. Romeo's mother made marvelous pasta and minestrone and dishes of mixed wild birds.

It was hard to leave, even for so great an attraction as Venice, where he was to meet Dr. Locke, who had generously offered to guide him through the museums and show him the Titians, the Tintorettos, and the Carpaccios. The sights were all he had dreamed they would be—the canals, the Rialto and the Bridge of Sighs, the unbelievably vast Piazza San Marco with its gay cafes and arcades and the Doge's Palace and the grand cathedral flanking it. But there was another side to Venice he found for himself—the back alleys crowded with poor people that reminded him of the slums back home.

Starting back to Paris by train, he fell asleep, and when he woke, his passport and wallet were gone. He had to get off the train at Genoa to seek help from the American consul. That gentleman said he could do nothing and suggested that Langston sign on a boat to work his way home.

For several weeks Langston slept in the municipal flophouse and went hungry while he tried to find work. But there was no work for Italians, let alone a stranded American. He bummed around on the waterfront with several other strays. Whatever these beachcombers lucked up on, they shared. He kept alive chiefly on spaghetti—it was very cheap—and a glass of red wine. Vagabond life sickened him after a while, and he tried to get away. But even here, thousands of miles from home, he got tangled up in the American color line. American ships came into the harbor and the white beachcombers were one by one signed on. But no Negroes were wanted. Langston had to wait until a ship with an all-colored crew showed up. The captain agreed to take him on as a workaway with no pay on the return trip to New York.

He chipped decks and washed paint as they sailed to Naples, Palermo and Valencia. Then they were past Gibraltar and out on the Atlantic. On the way across, he washed the chief mate's shirt for a quarter. They docked in Manhattan on a morning late in November and Langston caught the subway up to Harlem. Speeding through the dark, he sized up 1924. He had been away almost a full year, and had seen something of Holland, France, Italy, and Spain. He had worked hard when he could find a job, gone hungry often, fallen in love, and written several poems he could hope would last. He had reached Paris with seven dollars, and had come home with a quarter. Quite an education for only $6.75.

10   *Busboy Poet*

It was a big day for Langston, the day he came back to New York. He took his newest poem to read to his friends at a gathering in Harlem. There he saw Countee Cullen, whom he had met earlier. Just a year younger than Langston, Cullen had won recognition as a poet in high school and was now at New York University. Very different in temperament and style—Hughes, experimental, Cullen traditional—their names were already being coupled as twin stars among the new poets. There too he met another young poet for the first time—Arna Bontemps, the Louisianan who had been schooled out West and had just come to New York to teach, and who would become his closest friend. They left the party together, and walked home through the cold night, Langston freezing in his ragged pea jacket and wishing he had the money for an overcoat.

Going down to *The Crisis* office the next day, Langston found a double bonus waiting for him. They paid him twenty dollars for an article mailed from abroad, and showed him the November issue with one of his new poems:

> We cry aloud among the skyscrapers
> As our ancestors
> Cried among the palms in Africa,
> Because we are alone,
> It is night,
> And we're afraid.

Then they invited him to an NAACP benefit party at a Lenox Avenue cabaret. There he met James Weldon Johnson, one of the leading Negro writers, and Carl Van Vechten, the white writer.

He needed that overcoat badly, but he used the twenty dollars to go to the theater and to buy a train ticket to Washington. That city would be home now, for his mother—separated again from his step-father—had moved there. She and his brother

Gwyn were staying with cousins who were part of Washington's Negro society. They were the branch of the family directly descended from his grand-uncle, Congressman James M. Langston.

Langston was nervous about living with relatives —especially when he didn't have a dime—even though they were proud to have a poet in the family. But this might be his chance to go back to college. For now he thought it wasn't enough just to knock about the world; more education would also help his writing. There should be a lot to learn from sociology and history and psychology about the world he lived in and its people.

But where would he find the tuition money? He tried to get a scholarship to Howard University but it didn't come through. Then he looked for a job on which he could save up money for tuition. His cultured cousins felt being a page in the Library of Congress would be dignified work for a poet, but nothing came of that, either. Very broke—he owned nothing but his pea jacket, shirt, and pants— he took the first job that opened, in a wet-wash laundry.

He helped unload the wagons and sort the dirty

clothes for twelve dollars a week. It was impossible to save even a dollar toward college. Then they moved out of their cousins' home into two small unheated rooms, where, with his mother's low wages as a domestic worker, they barely scraped along.

Washington that winter was hard living. He was always cold and hungry. He hated his job but liked the people he worked with. He wrote "A Song to a Negro Wash-Woman," which *The Crisis* printed in January.

He was getting to know, too, the sour taste of Southern life. He had never gone deep into Dixie, but Washington was near enough to be a primer on Jim Crow, Southern-style. In Mexico and Europe he had lived, worked, and eaten with whites, and no one seemed the worse for it. Here, within sight of democracy's Capitol, ghetto life and laws were the rule.

When he asked why nothing was being done about it, Washington Negro society told him they couldn't be bothered, they had their own social world. He didn't think much of that world. It was filled with pompous gentlemen and puffed-up ladies who prided themselves on "family background."

These middle-class Negroes (few were really rich), lived as comfortably as they could and looked down on the folk who worked with their hands. If you hadn't been blessed with a college degree or your skin was too dark, you didn't count. To these snobs "black" was a fighting word.

Langston was fired by the laundry when he caught a bad cold and had to stay out a week. Soon he found a better place, however, in the office of Dr. Carter G. Woodson, founder of the Association for the Study of Negro Life and History, and editor of the *Journal of Negro History* and the *Negro History Bulletin*.

Dr. Woodson was leading the way for scholars to investigate both the African and the American past of the Negro. It sounded like a very promising job and it paid better than the laundry. But it turned out to be even harder work. Dr. Woodson was a remarkable man who made great demands on himself and expected everyone else to work the same way. Langston's job was to open the office early in the morning, keep it clean, wrap and mail books, help answer letters, read proof on the books and magazines, bank the furnace at night when Dr. Woodson was away, and do everything else the office girls couldn't do.

For several months he concentrated on alphabetizing thirty thousand names of free Negro families for one of Dr. Woodson's studies, and then checking and double-checking in manuscript and proofs to guarantee accuracy. It was an endless, blinding task, but he earned Dr. Woodson's compliments when he finished it. It finished Langston, too, however. If this was what they called a "position," he decided he'd rather have just a job. He quit to become a busboy at the fashionable Wardman Park Hotel. The pay wasn't much and the social standing it gave him even less, but it provided his meals and he didn't care about the rest.

What did matter was that one day he learned one of the leading poets, Vachel Lindsay, was staying at the hotel. He knew about Lindsay, that man who was minstrel and missionary both, a people's poet like Sandburg. Lindsay's rhythms too were influenced by the black man's syncopated music. Lindsay had gone up and down the country reciting his poems for a living, handing out a little pamphlet called "Rhymes to be Traded for Bread." Langston worked up his courage to the point of dropping three of his poems at Mr. Lindsay's dinner plate, unable to say more than that he liked Lindsay's poems and that these were his own poems. Then he fled toward the kitchen.

Lindsay gave a reading that night in the hotel theater, but the management allowed no Negroes to attend. When Langston showed up for work the next morning, reporters were waiting for him. They told him Lindsay had read his poems aloud and praised them to the large audience. The press interviewed Langston and took his picture. He was not really an unknown when this happened, for his work had already been published. But now his name spread overnight to the whole country. Newspapers carried the photo of the young poet in his busboy whites, toting a tray of dirty dishes. The Washington *Star* described him as "a quiet, earnest, rather gentle, diffident young man."

At the hotel desk Langston found that Lindsay, too shy himself to try to see Langston, had left for him a beautiful set of Amy Lowell's biography of John Keats. On the flyleaves Lindsay had written a long letter which said in part: "Do not let any lionizers stampede you. Hide and write and study and think. . . ."

The publicity was good for a young poet's career, but bad for his privacy. There was no place to hide.

Hotel guests would insist on Langston coming over to their table so that they could see what a real live Negro poet looked like. He couldn't stand that feeling of being in a zoo, and quit. For ten days he lay abed, just resting, tired of working, while his mother complained that *she* was tired of working, too. So he got up finally and found a job at a fish and oyster house downtown. It was a twelve-hour day, standing in a tall white hat behind a counter, making oyster stews and cocktails.

The year went by, an unhappy year, except for Saturday nights at the poet Georgia Douglas Johnson's home, where young black writers met to talk about their work, and the hours he spent hanging around dirty old Seventh Street. Here was the "low society" his cousins shunned, the people singing the blues, enjoying watermelon and barbecue, shooting pool, swapping tall tales. He would go to the shouting churches and listen to the gospel songs. It made him feel a little less bad about living in Washington.

But feeling bad had its good side, too. It meant he wrote poems. It made the misery more bearable if he could compress his feelings into the shape of a poem. He listened to Seventh Street's black music with its basic beat, the hand-clapping, feet-stamping, drum-beating rhythms which the Africans brought with them three hundred years ago. And in his poems he tried to catch the pulse of the blues with their one long line, repeated, and then a third line to rhyme with the first two. Sometimes the pattern shifted, with the second line changed a bit, or once in a while left out altogether.

On his way to work he would often write a blues poem in his head, singing it over and over again to himself to test the rhythm and to memorize the lines. Here is his "Bound No'th Blues":

> Goin' down de road, Lawd,
> Goin' down de road.
> Down de road, Lawd,
> Way, way down de road.
> Got to find somebody
> To help me carry dis load.
>
> Road's in front o' me,
> Nothin' to do but walk.
> Road's in front o' me,
> Walk . . . and walk . . . and walk.
> I'd like to meet a good friend
> To come along an' talk.

Hates to be lonely,
Lawd, I hates to be sad.
Says I hates to be lonely,
Hates to be lonely an' sad,
But ever friend you finds seems
Like they try to do you bad.

Road, road, road, O!
Road, road . . . road . . . road, road!
Road, road, road, O!
On de No'thern road.
These Mississippi towns ain't
Fit for a hoppin' toad.

All through the winter and into the spring of
1925 his poems continued to appear in the magazines. In March Alain Locke's Harlem number of
Survey Graphic carried more poems by Langston
than by any other writer. And almost on top of it
came the great news that his poem, "The Weary
Blues," had won first prize in *Opportunity* magazine's first literary contest. A Countee Cullen poem
had won second prize, and the judges awarded third
prize to both Langston and Cullen for other poems
they had submitted. Langston spent the forty-dollar
prize money on a trip to New York to attend the

awards dinner. He heard James Weldon Johnson read his prize poem aloud and met Zora Neale Hurston and Eric Walrond, prize winners for the short story and the essay.

In August he won two more prizes, this time awarded by Amy Spingarn through *The Crisis.* He visited New York again to receive second prize for an essay and third prize for a poem at a ceremony in the Renaissance Casino. He met Mrs. Spingarn and her husband Joel, a distinguished Columbia professor and critic.

Those trips to New York opened up new avenues for the young writer. He got to know many other Negro writers and artists—Aaron Douglas, Augusta Savage, Gwendolyn Bennett, Jean Toomer—and the editor of *Opportunity,* Charles S. Johnson. Johnson, he said later, "did more to encourage and develop Negro writers during the 1920s than anyone else in America." In Johnson's eyes, no other writer than Langston "so completely symbolized the new emancipation of the Negro mind."

Late in August came the grand climax. At the *Opportunity* dinner Langston had been asked by Carl Van Vechten to send along enough poems to make up a book. Liking what he saw, Van Vechten took them to Alfred A. Knopf, the publisher. Within a few days Van Vechten wired Langston: LITTLE DAVID PLAY ON YOUR HARP. Knowing it meant his book was accepted, he wired back: I AM PLAYING ON MY SILVER TRUMPET, OH SWEET JESUS.

In Washington he gave a reading of his poems arranged by Alain Locke. "It went well," he wrote his Knopf editor, partly because of the new aspect introduced—a blues piano interlude. Another reading was being planned for him in New York, and he suggested, "If you do get a real blues piano player to play, it ought to be a wow! But he ought to be a regular Lenox Avenue blues boy. The one we had here was too polished."

His letters to Knopf showed a concern for promoting his first book that would continue and grow more sophisticated. He supplied the names of newspapers, reviewers, bookshops, influential people he hoped the publisher would reach. And he arranged for his book to be on sale at his readings.

One day Langston met another young Washington poet, Waring Cuney, who was studying at Lincoln University in Pennsylvania. His college was a good place for writers, he told Langston. It was cheaper than Howard and left you ample time to write. So in October Langston wrote to Lincoln, saying, "I *must* go to college in order to be of more use to my race and America. I hope to teach in the South, and to widen my literary activities in the field of the short story and the novel."

He could not ask his father for money and, since his mother made little as a children's nurse, he would need work to help pay his way through college. His old high school in Cleveland recommended him to Lincoln, writing that he had been "one of the leading boys in the school," had "unusual ability" and "excellent personal habits."

Lincoln accepted him, giving him a semester's credit for his year at Columbia. He was to start in February. A year's tuition was $110 in those days, and with food, a room, and incidentals, his expenses would add up to about four hundred dollars.

But where would that money come from? Suddenly another opening to college appeared. Early in December Langston was told he might get a scholarship to Harvard if he tried hard enough and if he was "the splendid young man" the terms called for. He asked Mrs. Spingarn what she and her husband thought. "I know," he wrote, "that people are more interesting than books, and life, even a busboy's life, out of school, more amusing than a professor's in school. But I do want to be able to earn a little time for my own work (which I haven't now) and a little money for travel. So maybe I'd better try Harvard. . . ."

Mrs. Spingarn's answer came at Christmas time. It was the best present anyone had ever given him. Amy Spingarn told him she would pay his way through Lincoln. On December 29, he wrote to thank her:

I have been thinking a long time about what to say to you and I don't know yet what it should be. But I believe this: That you do not want me to write to you the sort of things I would have to write to the [Harvard] scholarship people. I think you understand better than they the kind of person I am or surely you would not offer, in the quiet way you do, the wonderful thing you offer me. And if you were the scholarship people, although I might have to, I would not want to accept it. There would be too many conditions to fulfill and too many strange ideals to uphold. And somehow I don't believe you want me to be true to anything except myself. (Or you would ask questions and outline plans.) And that is all I want to do—be true to my own ideals. I hate pretending and I hate untruths. And it is so hard in other ways to pay the various little prices people attach to most of the things they offer or give.

And so I am happier now than I have been for a long time, more because you offer freely and with understanding, than because of the realization of the dreams which you make come true for me. . . .

11   College Man

Lincoln was one of the oldest colleges established for men of color. A Presbyterian minister had founded it before the Civil War, in 1854. He thought it time that there should be at least one college where color didn't matter.

The college is set in the Pennsylvania hills about forty miles southwest of Philadelphia. That first spring Langston found the campus beautiful when the broad lawns came up green. Tall old trees stood between the faded red-brick buildings, and beyond them the quiet farmland stretched for miles.

There were hardly three hundred students at Lincoln then. All were Negro, although whites were welcome, too. The men (no girls were admitted) were from all over, including Africa. Some were the sons of the middle class and others the sons of working people. Many did chores on campus to help pay their way, and in the summers there was stiff competition for jobs at the resorts along the Eastern Shore.

Lincoln's white founder had been a Princeton man, and so were most of the faculty. For this reason and because the college was considered one of the best for Negroes, Lincoln men called it the "black Princeton." But the blackness was all in the student body. The faculty and trustees alike were white. Some Lincoln graduates were beginning to grumble about it. Francis J. Grimke, the distinguished Washington minister, had just publicly attacked the trustees for colorphobia, pointing out that in the school's seventy years they had never allowed a Negro on the board or the faculty.

In his stay at Lincoln, Langston took all the courses in American and English literature that were offered, always earning the equivalent of an A. He studied French, German, and Spanish, took economics, sociology, and government, and had a little math and science, as well as philosophy and ethics. In the study of the Bible—compulsory for an hour a week all through Lincoln—he was erratic, his grades beginning with a B, dropping to two Ds, and ending triumphantly with an A. He had said on entering that he wished to learn to teach, and his education courses actually outnumbered his literary, including two terms of practice teaching at the little public school in the neighboring village. At graduation his grades averaged a B-plus; he stood fifth in the class of forty-five.

He found some of the teachers very good, especially Professor Labaree, whom he remembered for knowing "how to put warmth and life into economics and sociology and race problems." But for several others he could say only that they were kind and well-meaning. Perhaps that accounts for his reputation as a chronic overcutter. Bored with lectures that added nothing to what he already knew or could learn less painfully out of a book, he would stop going. He was a good enough student, however, for his teachers to overlook his cutting. The fact that he was so much older and more experienced than the other students (he was twenty-four when he entered) may also have earned him forbearance.

Between students and teachers there was little give and take. The professors were to be seen only in classroom hours. Afterward, they retreated into their homes and left the dormitories and campus to the students. Unlike most Negro colleges, Lincoln did not impose rigid rules on social life. The men behaved any way they liked outside the classroom. Both Thurgood Marshall and Cab Calloway were among Langston's classmates. The future Supreme Court justice was the noisiest man in the class. He and Calloway could be heard "scatting jubilantly up and down the dormitory halls beating out rhythms on tin pans long after midnight."

When they had let off steam, the students subsided into bull sessions. There wasn't much else to do. Winters meant snowball fights, skating on the village pond, basketball in the barnlike gym, movies in chapel on Saturday nights. There were movies in town, too, but Negroes were segregated and few students cared to go.

Hazing was violent in those days. Because Langston had arrived on a wave of publicity over his just-published *Weary Blues,* the fraternity brothers were out to reduce this "big man" to his proper size. He was paddled so hard it was a week before he could walk normally.

An all-male student body was eternally on the hunt for girls. There were only a few Negro girls in the village. Young ladies were brought down from Philadelphia, Baltimore, New York, or the nearby Cheney Teachers College. There were never enough to go around.

In his second year Langston got deeper into school life. He wrote for the college paper, raced in the intramural track meets, and gave readings of his poems. That year one of the places he was asked to read was at a YMCA conference at Franklin and Marshall College not far away in Lancaster. The white students shared their dormitories and dining room hospitably with the Lincoln guests. At the working sessions they all talked about the national problem of Jim Crow in seeking jobs, in the Ys themselves, and in the churches.

On the last day, Langston thought it time to get down to something local and practical. He introduced a resolution to inquire into what seemed to be the host college's unwritten rule against admitting Negro students. But everyone seemed scared to take it up. In the end, the white Y director of the conference disposed of it by saying, "There are some things in this world we must leave to Jesus, friends. Let us pray!"

Langston wasn't content to leave such things to prayer alone. In his senior year at Lincoln he had to write a paper for his sociology class on some aspect of American life. He decided to do a study of the campus he lived on. His plan was to gather the facts on food, housing, social life, academic studies, and the relations between the black students and the white teachers.

In the back of his mind was the desire to dig into Lincoln's own peculiar color line drawn between students and faculty. He had heard some students say that white teachers were superior to black, and he set out to prove the college was creating feelings of inferiority in some of the very men it wanted to educate to be leaders of their race.

The survey showed that sixty-three per cent of the juniors and seniors preferred that Lincoln have an all-white faculty. The many reasons they gave all came down to a belief that blacks were somehow not as good as whites.

One way to overcome this, Langston suggested, was to appoint qualified Negro teachers. He named many to show they were available, and pointed to Fisk, with its mixed faculty, and Tuskegee, with its all-Negro staff. He underscored the fact that the courses of study at Lincoln completely ignored Negro history, art, and literature. Nothing was done to awaken students to an awareness of their past or the Negro's rich traditions of struggle and achievement.

His bold statement of the facts and his strong conclusions created a sensation on campus and off. One of Lincoln's celebrated old grads confided to him at graduation that you didn't get things out of white folks by telling them the truth. This man was a "success," but apparently he had become one by flattery and begging, by lying and by acting like an Uncle Tom.

Yet this was the kind of man the guest speakers at graduation told the students to look up to, men who shut their ears to the words of a Nat Turner or Frederick Douglass while they danced to a Jim Crow tune. He would run across many such, and one day would capture their inner conflict in his story "Professor."

Perhaps Langston was able to see what was wrong at Lincoln because he had gone through so much more than the others. Behind him was Mexico and Europe, and the experience of living more freely. What his survey revealed may have made a difference at Lincoln, for before ten years had passed many changes were made. Negroes joined whites among both faculty and trustees, and later on, whites entered to integrate the student body, too. Now the college even admits girls.

12   *Black Renaissance*

College life in a small town could not shut Langston away from the world. When the first summer vacation came, he went up to New York to seek work and to taste Harlem life again.

He rented a room in the house on 137th Street where the writer Wallace Thurman lived. To their place came many of the young leaders of the Negro Renaissance—Aaron Douglas, Zora Neale Hurston, John P. Davis, Gwendolyn Bennett. Langston's reputation had already been made with publication of *The Weary Blues*. The critics had hailed him as a poet "who played authentic blues with consummate skill." They used such words as "powerful," "sensitive," "warm," "lyrical," to describe his poems. *The New York Times* hoped he would receive "the wide reading he deserves," and the Washington *Post* said he "portrayed a deep understanding of the Negro heart and its aspirations." More than one critic compared him favorably with Carl Sandburg.

He had arrived, but his manner was so unassuming the people around him never felt in awe of him. They were all young, that year, all feeling for their roots, knowing they had something to say, not quite sure what it was. During the summer they got excited about plans to publish a Negro magazine of the arts to be called *Fire.* Their hope was to burn up the old outworn ideas of the past, and to light the way for the younger Negro artists and writers. Until very recently Americans had been quite unaware that there were any black artists worth paying attention to. But now Alain Locke's anthology had appeared in book form, swiftly stamping its name, *The New Negro,* on the decade of the twenties. This "new Negro" was not created by art. He came out of the millions who were on the move to the big cities. There they met new people, lived different lives. Old habits and customs fell away as they struggled for jobs and a place to live. Many worked for the first time in factories. Some entered law or medicine or teaching, or started their own small businesses. Massed in the back ghettoes, they learned to use the vote, and sensed the growing political power of their numbers.

It was a huge leap from a sharecropper's cabin to a Harlem tenement. Segregation and discrimination were still a daily and deadly pressure. But under it Negroes were compelled to build their own churches and newspapers and clubs, and they made their own music and literature. Through the arts they voiced their discontent and anger, and in speaking out renewed their race spirit.

Year after year new work appeared, each poem or novel shaped by a young writer struggling to express his own feelings in his own way, but all drawing encouragement from one another. James Weldon Johnson launched them, in a way, with his *Book of American Negro Poetry.* Then came the first individual books of poems—Claude McKay's *Harlem Shadows,* Countee Cullen's *Color,* and Langston's *Weary Blues.* The novel bloomed at the same time, with Jean Toomer's *Cane,* Jessie Fauset's *There Is Confusion,* Walter White's *Fire in the Flint,* Rudolph Fisher's *The Walls of Jericho,* and McKay's *Home to Harlem.*

Although the movement produced no serious

playwrights in the twenties, many superb Negro actors—Charles Gilpin, Paul Robeson, Rose Mc-Clendon, Frank Wilson, Abbie Mitchell—found important roles in Negro problem plays written by white dramatists such as Eugene O'Neill, Paul Green and DuBose Heyward.

Classical singers like Roland Hayes and Marian Anderson found it much harder to climb to the top, but still they succeeded. For popular musicians, however, the audiences seemed ready-made. Jazz—created by blacks and recognized the world over as America's most native music—came into its own in the twenties. Many of the great players and composers won their first fame then, and some, like Louis Armstrong and Duke Ellington, were still making music half a century later.

The burst of expression from Negro artists of every kind seemed to promise that the Negro would at last be fully accepted by America. James Weldon Johnson said, "Nothing can go further to destroy race prejudice than the recognition of the Negro as a creator and contributor to American life." There were many whites who agreed. Heywood Broun, a prominent newspaper columnist, believed that "a supremely great Negro artist . . . would do more than any other agency to remove the disabilities against which the race now labors."

Just to hear that hope expressed was a sign of progress. But many whites, picking up a book by a Negro writer, would still say, "Well, *some* Negroes are just as talented as *we* are." Great artists like Roland Hayes or Ethel Waters could receive standing ovations in the concert hall or theater and then spend hours in a despairing search for a meal or a hotel room. A display of talent was not enough to wipe out racial prejudice.

A summer hospital job that had been promised Langston fell through, but more happily he got the chance to work on the song lyrics for a musical revue. It was surprising, he wrote Mrs. Spingarn, to learn "how much understanding of human emotions there is behind a 'big' popular song—as trite as most of them are. Yet one has to have as exact a feeling for mood words to convey joy or sorrow or whatever it may be as one does in writing true poetry. I don't believe the work will hurt me any." It was his first of many experiences with the theater, and a great deal of fun. But, as would happen time and again, nothing came of it. The revue never reached the stage. There was talk of his writing the libretto for a Negro opera, but that too died out.

Far more serious was the work he put into his poems. Almost every night that summer he ground and polished one he called "Mulatto," trying to get it just right. At last he felt it was ready and the *Saturday Review* accepted it. It was the same theme of mixed blood that he returned to again and again.

From Lincoln he had submitted a poem, "A House in Taos," to the annual Intercollegiate Undergraduate Poetry Contest. News came that his was judged the best of the six hundred entries. The poem had come to him on the street one day. It was about a place in New Mexico's Indian country, a place he had only heard about but never been to. Different in form and tone from his other work of that time, it had thrust its way unaccountably into the midst of the blues poems he was writing. One of the poets judging the contest said the finding of this one authentic poet had made "all the other rot" endurable. The prize was $150. A little later the same poem won the twenty-five-dollar John Keats prize given by the magazine *Palms*.

The summer was gone before *Fire* was ready for the printer. It came out with flaming red lettering on a black cover, and a red lion crouched to spring. Two of Langston's poems were in it, "Elevator Boy" and "Railroad Avenue." *Opportunity* welcomed the new quarterly, calling it "a brave and beautiful attempt to meet our need for an all-literary and artistic medium of expression."

But most of the established Negro intellectuals, including Dr. Du Bois, detested it. The stories, poems, and drawings offended them. They were very sensitive to how the race was depicted in print. If whites were likely to read it—and a large part of the audience during the Black Renaissance was white —Negro critics wanted only the sunny side shown, the life of the educated, middle-class Negro who was a success.

They felt that way for good reason. Negroes were always being made fun of in the stories and cartoons of the popular magazines. The press made a sensation of every crime committed by or said to be committed by a Negro. Many a novel savagely caricatured the Negro, and, in the movies and on the stage, audiences saw Negroes only as clowns, servants, or helpless victims.

Langston's poems or Claude McKay's novels, honest though they were, were not welcomed. And when *Fire* appeared, with their kind of writing, the colored critics doused it with cold water. The first issue was the last.

Langston agreed that there was room for books

of the kind these critics wanted. But he didn't see why every black writer should be expected to produce such work. Feeling strongly about it, he wrote an essay which *The Nation,* an important magazine of opinion, printed that summer.

It read like a declaration of independence from the heart of Harlem:

> To my mind, it is the duty of the younger Negro artist . . . to change through the force of his art that old whispering "I want to be white," hidden in the aspirations of his people, to "Why should I want to be white? I am a Negro—and beautiful!"
>
> So I am ashamed for the black poet who says, "I want to be a poet, not a Negro poet," as though his own racial world were not as interesting as any other world. I am ashamed, too, for the colored artist who runs from the painting of Negro faces to the painting of sunsets after the manner of academicians because he fears the strange unwhiteness of his own features. An artist must be free to do what he does, certainly, but he must also never be afraid to do what he might choose. . . .
>
> We younger Negro artists who create now in-

tend to express our individual dark-skinned selves without fear or shame. If white people are pleased we are glad. If they are not, it doesn't matter. If colored people are pleased we are glad. If they are not, their displeasure doesn't matter either. We build our temples for tomorrow, strong as we know how, and we stand on top of the mountain, free within ourselves.

Standing on top of that mountain, Langston needed to be strong. For when his second book of poems appeared in February 1927, he was again pelted with stones flung by the Negro press. Most of the literary magazines liked the book, although some reviewers objected to its title, *Fine Clothes to the Jew*. The name came out of the custom of working people, when they were out of a job and broke, of pawning their clothes. They would say they were taking their clothes "to the Jew's." The title was a bad choice, and Langston regretted using it because it was so easily misunderstood.

One Negro paper called Langston the poet "low rate" of Harlem, and said his poems were "unsanitary, feeble creations." Another said the book was "trash from a Negro who writes mostly of the lower-class members of his race." The book "reeks of the gutter and the sewer," still another said, adding that "the world would be just as well off if poetry of this kind were unable to find a publisher."

Many of the poems were in dialect, and seventeen of them in the manner of the blues. They were not sentimental, but hard, sharp, vivid. They paid no heed to the conventional forms of verse. *Poetry* magazine's critic said they were "tragic cries and questions, prayers and hallelujahs, turned into poetry with an art and skill that makes them available to the experience of all." In the *New Republic* Abbe Niles suggested that the book "expresses the feelings of the porters, elevator boys, Harlem prostitutes and Memphis bad men into whose shoes he momentarily steps, with an explicitness and coherence which would be beyond most of them."

In her review in *Opportunity,* Margaret Larkin pointed out that Robert Burns had caught the dialect, speech cadences and character of the Scottish people in his poems, and said, "I think that Hughes is doing for the Negro race what Burns did for the Scotch—squeezing out the beauty and rich warmth of a noble people into enduring poetry."

Langston was not upset by the condemnation of

the Negro press, but he wanted to make his position clear. In an interview with the Pittsburgh *Courier* he said:

> My only fear is that the hostile attitude of our critics will frighten other younger writers away from writing about themselves. That would be a tragedy, indeed. The only true and lasting art that an artist can produce is that based upon what he himself knows best. I would certainly be out of my sphere if I attempted to write about the Vanderbilts or the Goulds or Park Avenue society, because I know absolutely nothing about those subjects. But I do know the humble side of Negro life, and that is what I have written about in my own way. At least two-thirds of our people belong to the lower class, and even I myself belong to that class, so why shouldn't I write about that class? Let some of those who know the upper class write about the upper class. I made it perfectly clear in my book which side of Negro life I was portraying, and it seems only sensible to me that I should be criticized for the way I portray it, and not for portraying it at all. I have a right to portray any side of Negro life I wish to.

13   *Not Without Laughter*

Like Vachel Lindsay, who had befriended him, Langston learned early that he could trade rhymes for bread. He had given the first public reading of his poems at the Community Church in New York in 1923. Then in 1926, just before entering Lincoln, he read his poems to a Washington literary circle under Alain Locke's auspices. With Lincoln as his base, he began to make many trips to read in cities north and west. He was paid for his readings, and the fees were important to him, but so was the experience of meeting his readers face to face.

Toward the end of his sophomore year, Fisk University invited him down to Nashville to read during commencement week. It was his first trip to the old South, and the first time he read his poems before so large a black audience. Their applause told him how close he had come to the heart of their common experience.

Fisk's fee was so generous he decided to spend it touring the South for the summer. Beale Street, the fabled street of those blues, was on his mind, and he headed for Memphis to see it. He was let down; Lenox Avenue in Harlem seemed just as colorful and colored to him. In the newspapers he had been reading about the Mississippi rising in the worst flood disaster in American history. Millions of tons of water had burst through the levees and drowned the homes of 750,000 people. Negroes and whites on the Delta plantations were fleeing before the raging waters. He went down to Baton Rouge to visit the huge camp set up for flood refugees. He learned that the whites had been taken down the river sheltered in steamers while the Negroes were put on flatboats open to wind and weather. There were government barracks for the whites, tents in ankle-deep mud for the Negroes. For whites, three meals a day; for Negroes, two. Negroes got the poorest issues of food and clothing. When workers were needed, Negroes in the emergency stations were herded into forced labor. They worked for nothing on the levees or for employers nearby who needed men. It was an old story for the black refugees; they had come from forced labor on the plantations.

Depressed by what he saw, Langston left for New Orleans, where he roomed on Rampart Street. His landlady held fish fries on Saturday nights and sold home brew. He spent hours listening to the wonderful blues records endlessly circling on her old Victrola, and picked up many of the verses he later wove into his own writing.

Down at the dock one day, the sight of a rusty old freighter made him ask again for a job going to sea. They signed him on as mess boy for a short round trip to Havana. Back soon in New Orleans, he had time to explore the old French Quarter before the summer was gone. Then he had to leave for Lincoln. On the way North he stopped at Tuskegee to talk about writing to the summer school students. In Macon he took a room in a colored hotel and found that Bessie Smith, the great blues singer, was staying there too. She was singing in the theater right next door. Her voice was so powerful he didn't have to go to the shows. He just sat at his window in the evening air and listened to her songs floating above the traffic and in between the buildings . . .

*I'm so downhearted, heartbroken, too. . . . I hate
to see that evenin' sun go down . . . You got a
handful of gimme and a mouthful of much oblige
. . . I love you, baby, but I can't stand mistreat-
ment any more . . . The mail man passed but he
didn't leave no news . . . Nobody knows you
when you're down and out . . . I hate a man that
don't play fair and square. . . .*

Those blues had been sounding in the hearts of
black folk for a long time. When Bessie Smith sang,
they came from all over to listen. Her big frame
standing solid on the tiny stage, her arms curved at
her sides, she would throw back her head and pour
the blues out.

Late one night Langston went out to look for
some barbecue and beer, which they shared, and she
told him, "The trouble with white folks singing
blues is that they can't get low down enough."

The next summer—it was 1928—Langston
didn't leave Lincoln's campus. He stayed in the
empty dormitory to work on his first novel. The idea
had been with him a long time. He wanted to use
his own childhood in Kansas as the root of a story
about a typical Negro family in the Midwest. But
to write it he needed time, a long time, and time

free of money worries. This summer he would have it, thanks to a very wealthy white woman a friend had introduced him to. She was Mrs. Rufus Osgood Mason, the very elderly widow of a distinguished physician. He called on her in her sumptuous Park Avenue apartment. There she held a salon open to promising young Negro writers and artists, often directed to her by Alain Locke. She usually placed her protégé on a footstool below her big chair, in which she sat like a queen in her purple velvet, crowned by her snowy white hair. She thought of herself as godmother to the young people of the New Negro movement, and liked to be addressed that way. When she learned Langston hoped to write a novel, she told him she would take care of his expenses so that he could have a free summer to work on it.

At first he had trouble getting started. His own family life and background was more unique than typical. But he had been poor like most Negroes, and he had seen a great deal of the family life of others. Two weeks went by and not a word on paper. Then he saw how to begin. His story became a mixture of true people and happenings, and invented ones. He felt his characters were coming alive. He charted their histories in notes pinned up all around his desk, and worked his way through a chapter at a time, revising it before going on to the next. That didn't turn out well, so he tried writing the novel straight through to the end without stopping to improve it. He finished the first draft with just enough time left for a short vacation on Cape Cod. Coming back to Lincoln for his senior year, he used all the time he could spare from his studies to work on the novel. Cutting. Polishing. Rewriting. All winter long it went on. He was no longer able to separate what had actually happened from what he imagined. The characters had their own life, talking to him, telling him what to write.

Graduation came, and the novel was still not finished. Given a generous monthly allowance by Mrs. Mason, he decided to stay on the campus, and by the end of the summer of 1929, the book was done. He went up to Canada for a holiday. But when he returned to New York, and read the manuscript again, it seemed dead. The life he was sure he had breathed into it had somehow slipped away.

He needed more time for it, and took a room in Westfield, a New Jersey town, so that he could work away from the distractions of New York. His window looked out on the little church Paul Robeson's father had built. On prayer-meeting nights he could hear the rhythmic sermons, the loud amens, and the fervent songs of the worshipers. He hammered at the novel all that winter. Almost two years had gone into it now. But at last he let it go off to the publisher. Then it was set in type, and proofed, and one day in July 1930, he saw it in the bookstore windows—NOT WITHOUT LAUGHTER, a novel by LANGSTON HUGHES.

The book was warmly received by the reviewers. One Negro critic liked it because it was "neither argument nor plea," but simply a story of "the average poor colored family trying to wrestle a living and some little happiness out of their unsympathetic environment. Their struggles, reverses, disasters, defeats and victories epitomize Negro life in the North and West." Another Negro critic said the novel established a new frontier for Negro literature. He praised Langston for staying away from the cotton field and the cabaret, and venturing into the hitherto unexplored region of everyday Negro life.

Several critics pointed out that the novel was weak in plot and structure, but rich in the creation of half a dozen contrasting characters whose lives were repeated by the thousands in America. And again, as with his poems, Langston was praised for giving the reader the very feeling and texture of Negro working-class life. Wallace Thurman, himself a novelist, called the book "an enviable first performance."

Why, then, did Langston say later, "I loathe this book—and never reread it—the only book of mine I do not occasionally open"? This was far more intense a dislike than he voiced in his autobiography, *The Big Sea,* where he said he "felt bad" because his novel wasn't good enough.

Writers often recognize that the result of their work hasn't come up to their hopes for it. But Langston showed so strong a feeling there must have been something more to it than a sense of technical failure. As though in apology, he said he had done the best he could, "under the circumstances at the time."

Without knowing much more than this, one can only examine these circumstances for clues. The part played by Langston's patron, Mrs. Mason, might account for his reaction. She not only financed the writing of the novel, but, according to *The Big Sea,* "read both drafts of the book, had helped me with it [one wonders how], and found it good." Not long after publication, however, Langston broke with his patron, in one of the most painful experiences of his life.

From the time he finished at Lincoln, Mrs. Mason

had made life very easy for him. "Out of a past of more or less continued insecurity and fear," he wrote, "suddenly I found myself with an assured income from someone who loved and believed in me." He thought Mrs. Mason was charming, delightful, brilliant, and wonderful company because of her familiarity with the arts and her friendship with all the great. He admired her too because of her generous gifts to so many worth-while causes, including the Negro's. He was flattered to be given so much of her time and attention. She bought him clothes, tickets for the theater, opera, concerts, lectures, and often went along with him.

"I was fascinated by her and I loved her," he wrote later. "No one else had ever been so thoughtful of me, or so interested in the things I wanted to do, or so kind and generous toward me."

This is in contrast, perhaps, with his own mother, who never seemed to appreciate her son's uniqueness as an artist. She seemed to be concerned more with how much money he made, and how much he could give her.

It all went wrong soon after *Not Without Laughter* was completed. He wanted to rest, to do nothing, to enjoy the good feeling of having finished a long and hard work. He was happy now, and couldn't write when he felt that way. But Mrs. Mason didn't understand. It was as though she had an investment in his talent and wanted to see it producing every minute she was around. Langston, tasting the easy life for the first time, wanted to relax and enjoy it. But much more than Mrs. Mason's pressure was interfering now.

The Great Depression had hit America only months after Langston had graduated from Lincoln. By the winter of 1930, five or six million were jobless. Homeless men were sleeping in subways and the hungry were begging in doorways. It felt uncomfortable, even shameful, to be living off Park Avenue bounty while almost everybody else was cold and hungry. He knew, too, that all that was keeping him off a breadline was his patron's whim.

On his way to Mrs. Mason's apartment, he often passed the new hotel on Park Avenue, the giant Waldorf-Astoria. Reading announcements about its ten-dollar dinners and ten-thousand-dollar suites, he got mad enough to write a poem he called "Advertisement for the Waldorf-Astoria." It contrasted the diamond-necklaced ladies enjoying the palace of luxury with the misery of the millions outside.

Mrs. Mason didn't like the poem. For months Langston hadn't written anything, and now, when he had, it wasn't what she considered beautiful. She thought Negroes were really primitive children at heart, and expected her protégés to live and write as though they were. But Langston knew he was a black American, with Kansas and Cleveland and Chicago and Harlem in him, not some noble savage of her imaginings. Their relationship withered and cooled until one day he told her he could no longer accept her money, although he wanted to keep her friendship and good will. She must have reacted violently, for Langston, in describing the scene later, could not bring himself to tell exactly what happened. Whatever she said or did, it caused him the same kind of deep emotional upheaval and physical sickness that had seized him in Mexico the day he realized he hated his father. He had believed all along that Mrs. Mason had liked him for himself, but was it only because she enjoyed the power to control his life? And now that he would no longer let her, she was enraged. Perhaps when she turned on him that day, she had revealed that her inmost feelings were rooted in racism. There is his statement that "in the end it all came back very near to the old impasse of white and Negro again, white and Negro —as do most relationships in America."

14 People Need Poetry

His patron's support had cushioned Langston against the first shock of the depression. He had come out of college trained to teach, but somewhere along the way he had given up that desire. Now that he had broken with Mrs. Mason, what would he do for a living? The fact that he had published poems, articles, and books had earned him prestige, but not money. He had never gotten more than seventy-five dollars from a magazine, and more often no reward but to see his work in print. His two books of poems had been critical successes, but hardly any poet's books reached more than five hundred or a thousand readers. His novel was new and its sales were as yet uncertain. Literary fellowships were very rare in those days and he could not expect to live from one to the next, the way some writers do today. There was no comfort to be had from the Harlem Renaissance movement, for it had fallen in the crash that brought everything else down. Most of white America was hit badly, and for Negroes it was worse. More than half of them were unemployed.

He could not trade his writing skills for a job in a publishing house or on a magazine. They would not hire Negroes to read or edit manuscripts. Nor did the radio networks or the Hollywood film companies welcome black writers. The only path open was to grind out cheap detective thrillers or Westerns for the pulps, or slick all-white romances for the higher-class magazines. It meant writing under a pen name, or trying to forget you were a Negro. He would not turn that way. "I wanted to write seriously," he said, "and as well as I knew how about the Negro people, and make *that* kind of writing earn for me a living."

It was a fantastic goal to choose. Few writers in America—amazingly few, considering the country's great size and wealth—have ever been able to make a living solely by writing what they liked. Almost all have had to take jobs to support their spare-time writing, or to find a working wife if they were not born rich. That is true of white writers, and the risk a black writer was taking was so much the greater.

Langston had already found this out, for writing had never supported him. He was twenty-eight now, and what had kept him going all these years? Working as a farm laborer, messenger, seaman, doorman, cook, clerk, waiter, busboy—but never writing. Yet he had the courage, or the foolhardiness, to make the decision to become a professional writer, and to stick to it.

Where would he begin? All he had to live on was the prize he had just won for *Not Without Laughter*. The novel had been given the Harmon Award for Literature—a gold medal and four hundred dollars. He sent a hundred dollars to his mother in Cleveland, and decided that with the rest he would go sit somewhere in the sun awhile. He thought of Haiti, for he wanted to write a play about the revolutionary days when the black islanders won their freedom.

With Zell Ingram, an artist friend from Cleveland, he headed South. Zell had borrowed three hundred dollars and a car from his mother. They drove through the late winter snows, uneasy as they reached the deep South. Only a few days earlier nine Negro boys had been accused of raping two white prostitutes on a freight train passing through Alabama. Almost lynched by a mob of white farmers, they had been put through a hasty trial in the town of Scottsboro that ended with eight of them sentenced to death in the electric chair. In the last year alone twenty-one lynchings had been recorded, and no one knew how many others had gone silently to their deaths.

At Daytona Beach they stopped to visit Bethune-Cookman, the college founded by Mary McLeod Bethune. Langston knew about this remarkable woman who had stayed in the South to create a school on whose campus no Jim Crow was permitted. When an artist like Roland Hayes sang there, the whites who wanted to hear him could come—if they sat side by side with all the others. It took gall and guts to defy law and custom, and she had plenty of both.

They arrived at night, and Mrs. Bethune welcomed them warmly with a room and a good meal. The next day she had Langston read some of his poems to the English classes. That night she sat up late with him to talk, sensing that he was floundering about, not knowing how to realize the goal he had set for himself.

But in her wisdom she saw that he had already

found the way, though he did not realize it. She pointed out how eagerly the students had welcomed him, how intent they had been on his reading, how proud they felt that a young black poet had earned a name in American literature. Don't you see, she said, that you make them feel they too can achieve something in this world, in spite of the color line?

He had been reading his poems to audiences in many places these past few years. But he had not stopped to think that, if you strung these audiences together in a planned tour, it could be made to pay. Added to money coming in directly from his writing, it might bring him a decent living.

Speeding down the Florida highway, he kept thinking about the prospect Mrs. Bethune had opened up. At Key West they took the boat to Cuba, where they stayed only a short while, enjoying the rumba parties and lobster suppers arranged by friends Langston had met on previous trips. Then they moved on to Haiti, that legendary country Langston had heard about from childhood. He had often been told by his grandmother the story of how Haiti became the first Negro republic in the world. His own great-uncle, John Mercer Langston, was part of Haiti's history, for in the late 1880s he had been appointed the American Minister to Haiti.

148

Negroes were so rare in the diplomatic service in those days that children were often named after his great-uncle. Even if Langston had not been related, he might well have been given the same name.

So he grew up on stories of Haiti. Its great leaders —Toussaint L'Ouverture, Dessalines, Christophe— were childhood heroes. And "freedom" became a wonderful word. He had heard from his grandmother how the Haitians, slaves to the French on their West Indies island, had fought Napoleon's troops for their freedom, and became the second free nation in the Western Hemisphere. (And in the example they set, a nightmare to the Southern slaveholders.) The Americans were the first, and they too had fought for their freedom, against the British. Revolutions, both of them. It made the word "revolution" a good word in his house when he was a child. And he had hunted through the libraries for every book about Haiti he could find.

Since leaving Lincoln he had been thinking about the need for stories and plays about Negro heroes. He had begun making notes for a play about the Haitian revolution. But before actually writing the play he needed to get the look and feel of the place. With Zell he spent six months in Haiti, most of it in the city of Cap Haitien, where the fabulous Citadel sits on its mountaintop. They stayed at a small hotel on the oceanfront, their window looking out over the harbor with its fishing boats. Langston spent many hours exploring the ruins of the Citadel, climbing up the rocky ledges that jutted out over the sea. The vast size of the Citadel was astonishing. To have built it in the days before bulldozers and cranes, getting the gigantic stones from the plain up to the lofty mountain peak must have meant an incredible human effort.

But what was left of that revolutionary legacy was sad to see. Haiti, when he was there, had for sixteen years been occupied by the U. S. Marines, there to make sure American investments paid off. It was the land of the shoeless people, a phrase Langston used to symbolize the extreme of poverty he found. In that stricken land a pair of shoes was enough to put a man in the upper caste. The vast majority of shoeless ones could not read or write, often had no jobs, and never had any power. The light-skinned were the upper class, the dark-skinned the lowly and scorned.

When summer ended they headed for home. On the way out they stopped at Port au Prince and Langston spent an hour with Jacques Roumains, the handsome, copper-brown Haitian poet. In a mixture of English and French they talked about poetry and people, and Roumains introduced him grandly to his friends as "the greatest Negro poet who had ever come to honor Haitian soil."

In Florida, they found the Ford needed repairs that took the few dollars they had left. They drove hungry the long miles up to Daytona. There they stopped again at Mrs. Bethune's to cash a check for the thirty dollars Langston had left in a New York bank. Mrs. Bethune was about to leave for Washington, and asked to ride along with them to save the train fare. On the road they stopped at a Negro school in South Carolina to have lunch with the teachers. At the sight of Mrs. Bethune classes were halted and an assembly called. She made a little speech and then introduced Langston. This young man writes poetry the whole South should know better, she said. He stood up and read some of his poems. The response was so enthusiastic it could almost have been a demonstration arranged to prove Mrs. Bethune's point.

"This is what you have to do," she said as they headed North again. "People need poetry."

15

Jim Crow, Southern Style

As soon as he returned to New York he began making plans for a poetry-reading tour. He would need several things—invitations from the Negro schools in the South, a car to get to them, and money to support himself until the bookings could do it. He wrote to the Rosenwald Fund, which had been set up by a multimillionaire to aid Negro education, and outlined his plan for a Southern tour. A thousand dollars was granted. He bought a Ford but, since he didn't drive, asked a Lincoln classmate, Radcliffe Lucas, to do the driving and act as manager, in return for half the profits of the tour. Lucas was glad to give up redcapping at Pennsylvania Station in those tipless times.

They worked out a series of letters to be sent to all the Negro schools and colleges. For the biggest ones, they decided to ask a fee of one hundred dollars plus board and lodging. It turned out several were willing to pay that much and sometimes even more. If a school pleaded poverty, Lucas would suggest seventy-five dollars, and if that proved too much, he would say that since they would be in the neighborhood anyhow, Mr. Hughes would make a special concession and come for fifty dollars.

In those depression days fifty dollars was a lot of money to many people. Langston was soon making lots of concessions. He would cut the fee to twenty-five dollars, or even give a free program "for culture's sake." They always put up a display of many books by other contemporary Negro writers, and sold copies of Langston's poems—the special edition of *The Weary Blues* or a twenty-five-cent printing of newer poems Langston had published himself.

This orange-and-black booklet he called *The Negro Mother,* after the fifty-two-line poem that would prove to be an audience favorite. He described the booklet's six poems as "ballads for recitation by amateurs in schools, churches, and clubs."

He also sold some of the poems as ten-cent broadsides suitable for framing or pinning on the wall.

They left New York on an October morning in 1931. First stop was a colored boarding school in Pennsylvania, where the youngsters gave Langston a big hand. So did the Morgan College students the next morning in Baltimore. He gained confidence as they moved farther South—Howard University in Washington, Union College at Richmond, Virginia State College, Hampton Institute . . .

Gradually Langston worked out an arrangement of poems that hardly ever failed to rouse his audience. If he did not hear a laugh or a sigh, applause or an "Amen!" he knew something was wrong. He always began by telling about his childhood and how he came to write poetry. Then he would read his earliest poems, written in high school, sometimes using verses in the Dunbar dialect style. They laughed at these, and at the jazz poems that followed. Later he would come to poems of a different mood, like "The Negro Mother," touching a deep family memory. Then he would get closer and closer to their own lives and problems. He read to them of porters, of housemaids, of elevator boys, of the chain gangs building the Southern roads, of sharecroppers and migrants and landlords.

Sometimes, as in "Song for a Dark Girl," he swung toward themes of violence, the violence that was an always present nightmare in the South:

> Way down South in Dixie
> (Break the heart of me)
> They hung my black young lover
> To a cross roads tree.

> Way down South in Dixie
> (Bruised body high in air)
> I asked the white Lord Jesus
> What was the use of prayer.

At the close of the program he would talk a little about race conditions, and then end with a poem he had written at eighteen:

> I, too, sing America.

> I am the darker brother.
> They send me
> To eat in the kitchen
> When company comes,
> But I laugh,
> And eat well,
> And grow strong.

Tomorrow,
I'll be at the table
When company comes.
Nobody'll dare
Say to me,
"Eat in the kitchen,"
Then.

Besides,
They'll see
How beautiful I am
And be ashamed—

I, too, am America.

Young people who heard him read his poetry in the South have recorded what the effect was. Addison Gayle, Jr., who became a college teacher, heard Langston when he came to his Virginia high school. The students had never met a live poet before, and Langston was a shock to them. "Even in that segregated school, our models for literature and success were white; and we were led to believe that a poet could only be white—tall with blue eyes and a shock of long black wavy hair." Emerson and Bryant and Wordsworth were the models presented by the teachers, not this short black laughing man.

They no more expected a Negro to be a poet than to be a President. Langston stayed a while after his reading, talking and encouraging them, destroying that distorted picture of what a poet was. And after his visit, many of the students began reading Negro writers for the first time—McKay, Johnson, Dunbar, Cullen, Hughes. They found, Gayle recalled, that the rivers Langston sang of were more real to them than those "limpid blue crystalline streams" that flow through so much of English and American poetry. His words had opened a new universe.

It went on that way for months on end. They had a booking almost every evening, and sometimes on Sunday afternoons, too. They drove hundreds of miles each week, bringing the poems to nearly every town and village in the South. No matter how small the place, if the folks wanted to listen, Langston was ready to read. His audience might be cotton pickers one night, and college students the next. He would be in a kindergarten today, and an old folks home tomorrow.

True Southern hospitality proved to be almost all black. With Negroes barred from hotels, the travelers had to stay in private homes. Each host, delighted to put up a guest of honor, would insist on keeping them up all hours to talk. They almost died of exhaustion and overeating. But they were not always in the hands of such warm friends. On the road the WHITE and COLORED signs popped up everywhere—on drinking fountains, in station waiting rooms, on toilets, in movies, over laundries, in restaurants, in parks.

They could never be sure when Jim Crow would appear, nor how great its cost might be. One weekend, at Hampton, news came that two Negroes, both on the staffs of Negro colleges, had just died tragically, the victims of racism. One, the dean of women at Fisk, had been injured badly in an auto accident in Georgia and had been refused treatment at the white hospital nearby. She died before she could be taken to the colored hospital miles away. The other, a coach on his way to see his football team play, had been beaten to death by an Alabama mob because he put his car in a white parking lot by mistake.

The Hampton students, horrified by the injustice, asked Langston to speak at a protest meeting on campus. He accepted, but the dean would not permit the meeting. Hampton did not like the word "protest," he said. That was not Hampton's way. Hampton believed in moving slowly, and quietly, with dignity. "We educate, not protest."

As Langston went deeper and deeper into the South, he became more and more depressed by the failure of the Negro colleges to fight against the color line. He found little personal freedom or freedom of expression on most Negro campuses for either faculty or students. Founded during the Civil War or after, the schools were beholden to whites for funds. "The tossed scrap of American philanthropy has bribed their leaders," he said. "The charity-luxury of Fisk, Spelman, Howard, fool and delude their students. Walk three blocks away from any of the famous Negro campuses and step into the mud of poverty and degradation up to your ankles. Ride ten miles from Tuskegee and see peonage." The schools were not trying to make men and women of their students, he thought; "they were doing their best to produce spineless Uncle Toms, uninformed, and full of mental and moral evasions."

This was the year of the Scottsboro case, but no one even mentioned the teen-agers sitting in their steel cages, waiting to die. Yet Scottsboro was a world-wide issue, challenging the way America treated its black minority. Langston wrote many poems about the Scottsboro boys, and read them across the South. One of them was "Justice":

> That Justice is a blind goddess
> Is a thing to which we blacks are wise:
> Her bandage hides two festering sores
> That once perhaps were eyes.

In North Carolina he was asked by the playwright Paul Green and the sociologist Guy B. Johnson to give a reading at the all-white university at Chapel Hill. Two students, editors of an unofficial campus literary paper, *Contempo,* heard he was coming and wrote to invite him to be their guest because the Carolina Inn, where university guests always stayed, would not house a Negro. The young editors wanted to show the world there were some white Southern students who didn't believe in the evil stupidities of segregation. Accepting, Langston sent them one of his Scottsboro poems, "Christ in Alabama." They printed it on page one of their paper the day he arrived.

> Christ is a nigger,
> Beaten and black:
> Oh, bare your back!
>
> Mary is His mother:
> Mammy of the South,

Silence your mouth.

God is His father:
White Master above
Grant Him your love,

Most holy bastard
of the bleeding mouth,
    Nigger Christ
    On the cross
    Of the South.

The white community was outraged. Within hours of the paper's appearance, tension was thick. Rumors flew that he would be run out of town. The sheriff said, "Sure he ought to be run out! It's bad enough to call Christ a *bastard*. But when he calls him a *nigger*, he's gone too far!"

Heavy pressure was put on the university authorities. A professor canceled the invitation he had given Langston to speak to his class. And Langston was refused the use of the music hall for his reading. He spoke instead in a smaller place, with the police standing guard outside as though they feared his words might spark a revolution.

The editors who had invited him were not frightened by the uproar. They defied custom further by taking Langston and several white students to a restaurant on the main street. They were allowed in because no one could believe a Negro would dare to enter. They assumed that the brown-skinned diner was a Mexican. When they found out the truth, they were furious.

News of the hullabaloo at Chapel Hill circulated swiftly through the South's newspapers. That was the end of invitations from white schools. Wherever he appeared next, the Negro audiences were overflowing, and delighted to meet a young man who had, they said, "walked into a lions' den and come out, like Daniel, unscathed."

At Tuskegee Institute, the school Booker T. Washington had built in Alabama, Langston was shown around by President Robert R. Moton, and the noted scientist George Washington Carver welcomed him to his laboratory. Langston read for an assembly, talked to the English classes, and visited with many students and teachers.

Tuskegee, he saw, was living in a strange half-world of compromise. Blacks staffed the Institute and the Veterans Administration Hospital, while whites owned the banks and stores and ran everything else, including politics, the courts, and the school system. The idea seemed to be, You blacks stay in your little world and we'll handle everything else. At the Institute, Langston was put into a student dormitory, where all Negro guests were housed. But visiting whites were put up in Dorothy Hall, a modern guest house for whites only, and were served breakfast in bed by the black students. In the town, no Negro, not even the famous Dr. Carver himself, could buy coffee or a soda in the drugstore. As for the ballot—porter or Ph.D., if you were black, you didn't vote.

As he moved about the campus, he heard not a word about the Scottsboro case. Yet only a few miles away, at Kilby Prison, the black boys were sitting in the death house. Their chaplain, a Negro minister, asked Langston to come and read to them. He did, choosing only lighter poems, saying nothing serious, except to hope the courts would soon free them. Only the youngest boy responded, smiling. The others sat silent and motionless.

To help rouse public support for the prisoners, Langston had written a short play in verse called *Scottsboro Limited*. It was printed in the *New Masses* in November 1931, and then he had it published as a booklet under that title, together with

163

four of his poems on the case. The play was given one performance in New York's Webster Hall that winter.

In the spring, Langston and Lucas headed west across the vast state of Texas, and over the desert through New Mexico and Arizona, on into California. Again and again they had trouble finding a place to sleep. Hotels and auto camps all across the country said, "We don't take Negroes." At Los Angeles, where nobody had ever seen a real live Negro poet, Loren Miller introduced Langston to an audience of 150 people as "the first Negro poet in America to span the continent with his poetry!"

In San Francisco he was invited to be the guest of Noel Sullivan, a wealthy white, at his home on top of Russian Hill, overlooking the beautiful city and the bay. He rested there from the hard winter of touring, and then undertook a month of lecturing.

In May a telegram came from New York asking him to join a group of Negroes heading for Soviet Russia to spend four months making a movie about the life of American Negroes. He was invited to go along as a writer, to do the English dialogue.

It was an offer that promised to open a new door. Negro writers had been given no chance to work in

Hollywood. Langston wanted to try his hand at every form of writing. If he was ever to write movie scripts, he would have to learn the craft outside the United States.

He wired yes, and then drove as fast as possible back to New York, stopping at Cleveland to see his mother and to leave her several hundred dollars. He barely made the boat, staggering up the gangplank with his bags and his typewriter, and his indispensable music—a stack of records and the Victrola to play them on. He might not eat in Russia (the country was going through a terrible famine) but he made sure he would hear his blues.

16 *Around the World*

It was an odd company to be sailing for the Soviet Union to make a movie. Only two of the twenty-two Negroes had ever set foot on a stage, and none had ever appeared in film. An attempt had been made to sign professionals, but when they learned they had to pay their own fare to get there, few would risk it.

Most of the group were just out of college, and not interested in acting careers. This was a miraculous gift—a free summer holiday at a time when jobs were scarce and money scarcer. Besides, it was a chance to escape from the color line back home and see a strange new world, a world where discrimination and segregation were said to be forbidden.

When they reached Moscow they were put up in

one of the best hotels in the heart of the Soviet capital and given special food privileges. A block away was the Kremlin, the center of Communist government, with ancient churches and palaces enclosed by a great wall. Russia's revolution was hardly fifteen years old, and the vast country was shaken by famine, epidemics, and a still chaotic system of production.

The film contracts were soon signed, Langston's paying a hundred times a week more than he had ever earned anywhere else. For a month they enjoyed the sights of Moscow while they waited for the movie script to be finished. When it finally appeared, the script was laughably out of touch with American reality. The Soviet writer had never been to the United States and very few accurate books about America had yet appeared in Russian. His story was a melodramatic treatment of the conflict between Negro and white workers and their bosses in Birmingham, Alabama. There was no denying that such conflicts existed, but the characters, the way they spoke and behaved, and all the details of American living were ridiculously wrong.

When Langston bluntly said so, the Russians were upset. They asked him to write a new script, but he said he couldn't because he didn't know the South well enough. While the Russians wrestled with the problem, the Americans were busy making friends and having fun. For weeks they made the rounds of theater and opera and ballet, went to concerts, receptions, and parties, tried out the few night spots, and gave interviews to the press and radio.

Just when the busy social life was beginning to wear them down, the film studio sent them south to Odessa, on the Black Sea. The plan was to shoot some cotton-picking scenes there. Nothing seemed to be ready for them here, either, so they passed the time loafing on the beach. Then one day the big holiday came to an end. The studio told them the picture had been dropped. There were anger and tears and even hysterics, with everyone voicing his own idea of what had gone wrong. Some charged there was a plot afoot to keep the world from seeing what kind of life American Negroes really lived. Others thought the picture had been abandoned because the Soviet government was on the verge of securing diplomatic recognition from America, and a movie exposing the oppression of American Negroes wouldn't help. Langston said he didn't think a decent film could have been made from the script, anyhow, and if the group had done it they would have ended up ashamed of the picture. He felt it was wiser to make no picture at all than a bad one.

The Russians did their best to ease the disappointment, paying out the contracts in full, and the round-trip fares, too. They allowed anyone to tour the country or even stay permanently, if he wished. Some of the Americans left for home, others for western Europe, and a few chose to stay on for good. Langston decided to see more of the Soviet Union. Back home, where America was still floundering badly in the third year of the depression, people wanted to know if Russia had found the way to end unemployment and hunger. So did Langston, but he was even more interested in finding out the place of the Soviet Union's colored peoples under socialism. He got permission to travel as a reporter to Turkmenistan in Central Asia, where most of the brown-skinned Asians lived.

On the long trip, the Russians aboard his train entertained with mandolins, balalaikas, and accordions. Langston, who couldn't sing, played them records on his Victrola. The Russians, like everyone else around the world, loved American jazz. "A good old Dixieland stomp can break down almost any language barrier," he said. "There is something about Louis Armstrong's horn that creates spontaneous friendships."

Turkmenistan turned out to be largely desert, with less than a million inhabitants, most of them seminomads. The others lived in the few scattered towns, where factories were now springing up. In the sleepy old town of Ashkhabad there was no hotel, only a hostel for visiting officials, where he was put up. He lay on his iron bed, waiting for someone to take him to dinner, and dozed off while a Louis Armstrong record ran down on his Victrola. A bright-eyed young Oriental in a Red Army uniform knocked and came in. He talked fast, in a musical-sounding tongue, but Langston couldn't understand a word. Nevertheless they wound up going out to dinner together, with the soldier still talking on, and Langston beginning to answer in English—a conversation in which neither ever knew what the other was saying. The furthest they got was to learn each other's name. But they saw each other for weeks, becoming as close as brothers. They went to the circus often and dated girls together.

The weeks were slipping away without any work getting done. Langston's conscience might have shamed him into writing if a new arrival had not done it faster. It was Arthur Koestler, a young white writer reporting for German newspapers.

Staying in the next room, he had heard Sophie Tucker singing "My Yiddishe Momma" on Langston's Victrola, and had knocked on the door to find out who his neighbor was. He was delighted when it turned out to be Langston Hughes, whose poems he had read and admired in Berlin. Later, in his autobiography, Koestler said of Langston: "Behind the warm smile of his dark eyes there was a grave dignity, and a polite reserve which communicated itself at once. He was very likable and easy to get on with, but at the same time one felt an impenetrable, elusive remoteness which warded off all undue familiarity."

When Koestler learned Langston had yet to make a single note on what he had been seeing, he reminded him that "a writer must write." He suggested they combine forces and travel through Turkmenistan together.

Aided by local officials, they visited cotton plantations in the irrigated regions and textile mills in the towns, went to meetings of workers' councils, inspected schools and factories, and saw experimental agricultural stations. Langston even discovered a film school, recently opened, that trained illiterates from the regional nomad tribes to read and write while they mastered all the skills of making movies. In the eyes of an American Negro, it was strange to see colored Asians being taught by Russian whites how to make films from the ground up, while in Hollywood a brown skin permitted you only to sweep studio floors.

Koestler saw this and many other things in Soviet Asia differently from Langston. Racism was not uppermost in his mind. Hitler had not yet stamped his brand of Aryan superiority on the Germany Koestler was now living in (although it would happen within months). Trained to highly developed European standards of work and discipline, he was upset by the dirt and inefficiency he saw all around him. A member of the German Communist Party, he regretted that the revolution had not happened first there, where "at least it would have been a clean one," he grumbled to Langston.

Langston tried to make him see that, in a Negro's eyes, the fact that equality had been won for the colored Asians was far more important than that a roomful of people drank out of a common tea bowl or a hotel room was filthy.

Once, when they were talking about the Communist Party, Koestler asked Langston why he had never joined it. He answered that jazz was officially banned in Russia as decadent capitalist music, and he wouldn't give up the music he loved for any revolution. It seemed a minor point, but it led into the bigger reason he gave: that the Communist Party demanded strict discipline of its members, and as an artist he could not follow orders blindly. He needed the freedom to write whatever seemed true to his own feelings and beliefs. He did not believe political leaders should shape or limit an artist's work. Koestler did not try to argue him out of his position, and some years later himself quit the Communist Party.

Taking roads that often followed old caravan trails, they wandered through the heart of central Asia. From Ashkhabad they went to Bokhara, where they lingered in the old city for weeks. At Tashkent, the next stopping place, Koestler left for Moscow. The next time Langston saw him, many years later, Koestler was a world-famous novelist. Langston stayed on in Tashkent. He collected six thousand rubles as an advance from the government publishing house, which was having his *Weary Blues* book translated into Uzbek. Negro life in America might seem remote from this Uzbek land, but under the Tsars the Uzbeks had been treated by the Russians with the same discrimination Negroes met back home.

It was handsome payment for his poems— enough to buy thirty camels!—and he would have been jubilant if he had not felt so sick. He flopped into his hotel bed, bones aching, so sick he couldn't eat. A group of Tashkent writers who looked him up saw how ill he was and arranged for him to be cared for.

As soon as he recovered, a translator was assigned to him, and he went about interviewing people again for articles. Once he drove an hour out of Tashkent to where crews of young men were ex- cavating for the building of an enormous power dam at Chirchikstroy. As night fell they reached the raw wooden barracks thrown up to house the con- struction workers. Tajaiv, a brown-skinned Uzbek youth, came up to Langston to welcome him. He spoke proudly of how he and the young workers had built these first barracks to live in while the dam was going up, doing it in their spare time as a special contribution. He was helping to bring light and power and chemicals to this huge part of his once backward Asia.

Tajaiv seemed to Langston the symbol of what the young U.S.S.R. was trying to do. In Turkistan the revolution was only ten years old. Describing the days before the old life was uprooted, Langston wrote:

A brown young Uzbek like Tajaiv would have had to ride in the back of streetcars in Tashkent, for previous to the revolution in Asia there had been Jim Crow streetcars in Uzbekistan. The old partitions that once separated natives from Europeans, colored from white, were still there when I arrived—I saw them. But now anyone sat anywhere in the Tashkent trams. In ten short years, Jim Crow was gone on trams, trains, or anywhere else in Central Asia. Russians and Uzbeks, Ukrainians and Tartars, Europeans and natives, white or colored, all went to the same schools, sat on the same benches, ate in the same co-operatives, worked in the same shops or factories, and fussed and fumed at the same problems. Gains and defeats were shared alike. In Tashkent, whenever I got on a streetcar and saw the old partitions, I could not help but remember Atlanta, Birmingham and Houston in my own country where, when I got on a tram or bus or a train, I had to sit in the COLORED section. The natives of Tashkent, about my own shade of brown, once had to sit in a COLORED section too. But not any more. So I was happy for them.

The changes were being made at great cost, he knew. Those who didn't like it were almost all in jail, or dead, often executed. Life in Tashkent was far from perfect. Only the people at the top— political bosses, scientists, engineers, managers, artists—knew comfort. And not even they knew safety or security, for political trials and purges were already taking a savage toll. Still, he felt life for most of the people must be better than it had been in the days of serfdom and Jim Crow. The unanswered— and perhaps unanswerable—question was, could it have been made better by less violent and more democratic means?

Six months after he had gone into Asia, he was back in Moscow. He got a room and went to work on articles about his trip. He was paid very well for them by Russian publications. He decided that when the time came he would use the money to go eastward around the world, reaching home by crossing the Pacific.

He made the rounds of the theaters again (more

than sixty were active) to see all the current productions, and met several of Russia's leading writers. Among them was the poet Boris Pasternak (much later to become known around the world for his novel *Dr. Zhivago*). Pasternak refused to write political poems to please the authorities, risking official disgrace. Langston liked the tall, gentle, shy man.

Winter nights in Moscow could drop to twenty below zero, but so long as he had a bed and enough to eat, Langston could get along anywhere. Other American travelers complained about the bad food, the high prices, the jammed streetcars, the infuriating indifference of clerks and waiters, the damp, chilly apartments. Many of the visitors from abroad came starry-eyed to this land of their dreams, but found the reality too grim to tolerate.

While he was waiting for a permit to travel across the Soviet Union to the Pacific, a visiting Englishwoman lent him a copy of the short stories of D. H. Lawrence. Langston had never read him before. Nothing more important happened to him during all those months in Russia. Lawrence could strip the skin off his characters and reveal their inmost heart to the reader. Langston was shaken by the English writer's power, especially in his "The Lovely Lady," a story which dissected an old woman who was terrifyingly close in type to Langston's Park Avenue patron. Lawrence portrayed her as a woman whose well-preserved beauty was like armor shielding something hideous and evil inside. She could love nobody, not even herself, only her power to feed on other lives. Even reading about someone like Mrs. Mason was still almost too much for Langston to bear. But the shock of Lawrence's creative imagination made him want to try his own hand. He had yet to write short fiction, although *Not Without Laughter* reads more like a chain of short stories connected through the same characters than like a novel. Lawrence was so compelling an example to him that he dropped his journalism at once and tried instead to draw up out of his own experience stories that would make his readers, too, sweat and shiver.

Two nights after reading Lawrence he sat down and began to write stories. The first few, which he showed American friends living in Moscow, all dealt with the relationship between a young Negro and his art patron. Then he veered off and wrote "Cora Unashamed." It had begun in his mind with the facts a friend had once told him about a pretty Negro girl who had died of an abortion. But his own experiences, his own personal way of looking at life, took over, transforming the details of the original into something very different, something uniquely his own creation. It became a story about Cora Jenkins, an old Negro housekeeper who has slaved long years for a middle-class white family in a small prairie town. The conflict is between Cora's human values and the Studevants' cold indifference to life, even when it is their own pregnant daughter's life at stake.

Once started, Langston kept on working through the spring. The first three stories he mailed off were bought by major magazines in New York, and "Cora Unashamed" was selected for O'Brien's *Best Short Stories of 1934.*

When summer came, he took the Trans-Siberian Express across the endless stretches of land and at the end of ten days was in Vladivostok, a dismal, damp, and dirty town that looked like a frontier post. There he boarded a boat for Japan. He explored Tokyo for a few weeks and then moved south to Shanghai, on the China coast. The Japanese, already moving in on China, had begun to take over the many rackets that operated in Shanghai, from prostitution to narcotics. In 1933 the huge multiracial city was an armed camp, with brutality and death everywhere. The year before, thirty thousand corpses of the poor and homeless had been picked up on the streets.

Jim Crow was the law here. The white foreigners who had dominated Shanghai for so many years built barriers around the Chinese right in their own country. Langston found he could not stay at the "white" YMCA or at the hotels in the International Settlement. The clubs of the British and French were open only to whites.

The worst sight he saw was the Chinese children slaving in the textile mills. As soon as they were big enough to stand at a machine, their starving parents gave them to labor contractors for a small payment. The children would disappear into the mills for as long as ten years, sometimes never to come out alive. They worked twelve hours a day and slept in the company dormitories at night. In one mill Langston visited he saw two hundred boys and girls from ten to sixteen years of age working wearily at the looms. It might have been a Carolina mill back home—the same stunted bodies, the same worn faces, like little old men or women, the same hopeless eyes.

Shanghai was a sprawling mass of four million

but he did his best to get a look at them all. White Westerners warned him not to go out of the International Settlement at night. Of course he did, and nothing ever happened to him. He walked the odd-smelling exotic streets from the Bund to Bubbling Well Road. He saw the race tracks and theaters, the amusement parks and gardens, the shops and markets. He met people of all colors and tongues.

Some of the liveliest hours he spent with folks from back home—the Negro musicians and entertainers working in Shanghai's clubs. Wherever he might be, he was drawn to show business. If a choice had been possible, he might well have preferred to be a performer, not a writer. But he was a writer, and he couldn't afford to stay too long in the Orient. A Japanese ship carried him across the Pacific into San Francisco Bay, where fifteen months ago he had started on the trip that had taken him all the way around the world.

17 *Dream Deferred*

While Langston had been away in Russia and Asia, America had sunk to the bottom of the depression. Seventeen million workers were unemployed. And writers shared in the common suffering. Erskine Caldwell, for instance, leaving a hungry family of four in Maine, had come down to New York with ten cents in his pocket, sleeping nights in a hallway while he looked for work. By the end of 1932 the country seemed to be slowly strangling to death. Thousands of banks had gone under and a million farmers had lost their farms. Bread lines and soup kitchens were everywhere. The Hoover administration in Washington did almost nothing to provide relief. It believed the country was "fundamentally sound" and would work its own way out of the crisis. Then, in March 1933, Franklin D. Roosevelt took office. The new President sensed that after years of hunger and demoralization the people wanted action. He did not fear to experiment, to break the rules, to do the unprecedented. That spring he put dozens of new measures through a willing Congress. Federal funds to relieve the suffering came first, then programs to create jobs for the unemployed. Public works were launched on billions of New Deal dollars.

By the time Langston landed in San Francisco, the fog of hopelessness was beginning to lift. Jobs had been created for over two million of the unemployed. Many millions more were still without work, but at least they had hope. There was even talk of creating public works projects that would put to use the talents of unemployed writers, artists, actors, musicians.

Langston debated whether to go back to Harlem. But what could he do there? The depression had hit Negroes even harder than whites. One out of three whites were unemployed, but one out of every two blacks. And he wanted to go on writing. He had hit his stride with his short stories, and hated to stop now. At Noel Sullivan's house, where he had been made welcome again, he told his host he hoped to produce enough stories for a book. Sullivan generously offered him a cottage he owned at Carmel, down the coast. He could have it rent-free for a year.

It was an oasis for him in the desert of the depression. He would have his peace and security, and some of the money his stories might earn he could send home. His stepfather had wandered off again, leaving his mother and brother in need of help.

At Carmel he learned he could have as much social life as he wanted, for the seaside village was a haven for writers and artists. Among his closest friends were the veteran journalist Lincoln Steffens and his wife, Ella Winter. He joined with them and many others in the protest movement rising rapidly on the West Coast. They took sides in the battles of the unemployed, of the migratory workers, of the Spanish-Americans and the Negroes for jobs and for justice. They wrote leaflets and helped distribute them, they sent letters and signed petitions, they joined picket lines and demonstrations, they went on delegations to relief stations and the state capital. Writers could do this, but they could do more. They could speak the truth, and by their power of eloquence help others to see it.

They were alarmed by the rise of fascism in Europe and Asia and the failure of the democracies to do anything to stop it. The world had stood by while Mussolini conquered Ethiopia and the Japanese took over Manchuria, while Hitler marched into the Rhineland and then into Austria. Few people could bring themselves to believe in the reality of Hitler's concentration camps and tortures or in his elaborate and public plans for world conquest. In January of 1935, when a group of writers issued a call to form an organization "to defend culture against the threat of fascism and war," Langston Hughes and Richard Wright signed their names to it. Later, unable to attend the first American Writers' Congress in New York, Langston sent a speech to be read for him. It was an appeal to Negro writers to help unite blacks and whites, "not on the nebulous basis of an inter-racial meeting, or the shifting sands of religious brotherhood, but on the solid ground of the daily working-class struggle to wipe out, now and forever, all the old inequalities of the past."

Now and then friends came by to use the cottage's extra bedroom. Once Roland Hayes stayed a few days while on tour, and Wallace Thurman, his old Harlem friend, now writing Grade B movies in Hollywood under a "white" pen name, dropped by for a weekend. Thurman, more bitter and unhappy than ever, was already ill with tuberculosis, the disease that would end his life in a charity ward in New York barely a year later. Thurman was like many other writers he knew—deeply unhappy, never content with their lives or the world around them. That was how Arthur Koestler had struck Langston, and he sensed this in Richard Wright, too. Their spirits were restless, uneasy, always hunting for something not there. But their sadness did not turn him away. Rather he was drawn to people emotionally distressed, knowing what they were feeling because often he too had the blues. But he held them so deep down that his friends could rarely feel it.

That fall he wrote a lot, putting in ten or twelve hours a day. Almost every week he was able to finish a story, and sometimes more than one. He was at his best when the task he set himself was short. He could get the shape of the story blocked out in a swift draft and then work it over until he felt its details were right. He sent the stories to the magazines as he went along. It wasn't easy to get them published. One of his best known, "The Old Folks at Home," a story about racial violence in the South, was originally sent to the *Atlantic Monthly,* an old and highly regarded magazine. The editor turned it down with a note that said: "Why is it that authors think it is their function to lay the flesh bare and rub salt in the wound?" The story, he went on, "is both powerful and delicate but we cannot forget that most people read for pleasure, and certainly there is no pleasure to be found here." But *Esquire* took it.

Soon he had enough stories to provide a book. In mid-1934, Knopf published fourteen of them under the title of *The Ways of White Folks.* Most of the stories were about the impact of whites and blacks upon one another, with whites holding the controlling hand. Black workers were often the center of the story—sharecroppers, domestics, book-keepers, laborers, janitors—and the theme was the way they were exploited by whites. He cut both ways with his irony, scorning the fake friendship some patronizing whites offer to Negroes, and de-ploring the Uncle Tom humility some Negroes dis-play to whites. A theme that ran through several of the stories was the wall the Negro eventually ran into, no matter how far his talent or energy or skill might have carried him. Sooner or later, the stories demonstrate, the white folks will try to force him to stay within the "nigger" character they have defined for him.

Langston decided to break the stay in Carmel by crossing into Nevada to see what Reno was like. He had heard it was a stopover for the huge army of Americans roaming the country in search of work or a handout. Riding the rods from town to town, the homeless migrants would hole up for a while in the big hobo jungle on the edge of Reno. Langston visited it, and talked with many hungry Negroes stopping there. "The Biggest Little City in the World," as Reno advertised itself, was also big with prejudice. Negroes could eat in no public places except for two beaneries owned by Chinese, and at the city relief shelter they always said, "The beds are all gone," when a black man appeared at the door.

Langston took a room in a Negro boardinghouse —the owner was on relief, like most of the tenants —and shared the home relief suppers. He worked hard every day on stories suggested by the misery he saw around him. One of them, "On the Road," was a powerful fantasy about the adventures of a Negro hobo who meets a Christ dispossessed like himself.

He wrote it in one sitting, the way he wrote a poem. It is one of his best stories.

In the late afternoons, tired of pounding the typewriter, he would go for a long walk. One day at dusk he came to a little mountain cemetery, with a few lonely graves. From the distance he could see a mailbox on the cemetery gate, although there was no house around. That's strange, he thought—a mailbox for the dead? But when he reached the gate, he saw it was only an old board that had warped and buckled into the silhouette of a mailbox. Walking back to the boardinghouse the phrase "mailbox for the dead" excited him, and he began imagining a situation to fit the title. That night he sat down and roughed out a story. As he worked, his father kept coming into his mind. It was thirteen years since he had last seen him in Mexico. They had written each other perhaps two or three times a year in all this while. A long time often passed without Langston ever thinking of him. Maybe I ought to write him now, he thought. But he went to bed. The next day word came by wire that his father had died, and at the very time that Langston was writing "Mailbox for the Dead."

The telegram said the reading of the will would

be delayed until Langston could arrive in Mexico City. He was sure his father had left him nothing. When he got there, he found his name had not even been mentioned in the will. It did not surprise or disappoint him. There had been no love between himself and his father, whom he had seen only twice in the thirty years James Hughes had lived in Mexico. His father left his property to three elderly and devout Mexican ladies, unmarried sisters who had long been among his few friends and who cared for him in his last years when he had been partly crippled by a stroke. The three sisters wanted to share the estate with Langston, dividing it four ways, but he said no, his father obviously had not wanted that.

Now that he was there, why not stay in warm Mexico through the winter? Besides, he had to earn enough money to pay his way back home. He loved Latin America and the Spanish language and it was easy to make the decision.

Soon he was able to earn some money by translating into English the stories and poems of many young Mexican writers he met. In turn, they asked his help in translating the syncopated rhythms and Harlem slang of his poems into Mexican idioms and Spanish meters. He made friends, too, with some of the country's great artists—Rivera, Siquieros, Orozco—who were creating a style of mural painting, using Mexican history and folk themes, that was attracting world-wide attention.

Langston shared a small flat near a marketplace with the young French photographer Henri Cartier-Bresson and a Mexican poet, Andres Henestrosa. They had very little money among them, but what difference did it make? Langston wrote and sold a few stories, Cartier's pictures were just beginning to be shown, and Andres, an Indian from Oaxaca, was transcribing folk tales and creating the first dictionary of his own Indian language. After the day's work they were busy courting. Andres was in love with a beautiful dark-brown Indian girl whom he later married, Cartier with another Indian girl who went about barefooted, and Langston with Aurora, the daughter of a tortilla maker.

When there were no parties to go to they spent the evening loafing at the little bars and clubs, listening to the mariachis' guitars and their wailing voices. When they were broke, and they often were, they went hungry. But they didn't worry or care. They lived amid thousands of very poor people in the heart of Mexico City. And Langston was long used to living hand to mouth. That winter and spring were the nearest he came to living the bohemian life.

When summer came, he went back to California to work on a children's book about Mexico with Arna Bontemps, his old friend. Earlier they had written together a children's story of Haiti called *Popo and Fifina.* The Bontemps family was living in a little house in Watts, then on the edge of Los Angeles. The two writers were broke, and jobless, trying to get by on the little their writing brought in. They finished the book but no publisher would take it in that dismal time when turndowns were the order of the day for so many manuscripts. They tried another book, and it suffered the same fate. Langston was staying with Arna's aunt in a bungalow across from Jordan High School. Almost every evening they would walk into the heart of Watts, often with Arna's youngsters, and console themselves with giant ice-cream sodas. Then Langston heard from his mother that she was very sick (it was cancer of the breast) and had no money. She had moved to Oberlin in Ohio to live with distant cousins.

He left Watts and went to see his mother. When he got there he didn't wonder that she had no money. She had been helping the newly discovered cousins, who had even less. As often as he sent her money, it was never enough, for she kept handing it to all the relatives around her. Like many other people, she couldn't believe that a writer of books didn't make much money. He tried to explain to her that, although his own books were praised by the critics, they were far from best sellers. There was often a big gap between the sale of one story and another. Royalty checks were pitifully small during a depression when few people could buy the food they needed, much less a book.

But, his mother would say, if writers don't make decent money, why don't you just quit and get a job? Sometimes he felt gloomy enough to agree with her. But where, in these times, could he find a job that would support his mother, his brother, and himself? As her illness got worse, it took every penny he could earn. The Guggenheim Fellowship he won that year, granted to support his writing, went mostly to pay his mother's doctor bills.

He stayed awhile in Oberlin, working at stories and articles. During that summer the federal government expanded its work relief by adding several arts projects. National programs got under way in the theater, music, painting, writing, the dance. Thousands and thousands of artists, writers and performers, idle for years, went gladly back to work. Thin as Langston's income was from writing and lecturing, it was enough to disqualify him from the WPA projects. Workers were taken only from the relief rolls.

In the fall he decided to go to New York to try to sell his stories. When he arrived, he was astonished to find that *Mulatto,* a play he had written six years earlier, was in rehearsal for a Broadway opening. This was his first major play. Shortly after graduating from Lincoln University he had spent some time at the nearby Hedgerow Theatre managed by Jasper Deeter. There, working at his usual swift pace, he wrote *Mulatto* within a few weeks. Deeter had intended to present it that fall with Rose McClendon in the mother's role, but when she was engaged for a Broadway play, the project was dropped, and Langston had gone back to completing work on his novel.

The play's theme was one that had drawn Langston again and again—the problems of the Negro with mixed parentage. It was in his 1925–26 poems, "Cross" and "Mulatto." And after writing the play, while living at Carmel, he had converted its action into a long story he called "Father and Son."

He wrote the play as a poetic tragedy about the son a plantation owner has by his Negro housekeeper. The colored son and white father, looking at the South through very different eyes, clash, and the father is killed by the son. When a lynch mob comes after the boy, he kills himself, and his mother is driven insane.

Langston's agent had not bothered to tell him that a producer named Martin Jones had bought the play. Now, after signing the contracts, he went down to the theater to watch rehearsals. The actors were reading many lines he couldn't recognize. It turned out that Mr. Jones had made changes to suit his own notion of what was "box office." To him, playwrights were just a nuisance he had to put up with. They supplied the raw material, which he processed into a profitable product. He told Langston to sit down and watch.

He did, and found he was repelled—and fascinated. The producer had made many changes to sensationalize a play that already had its quota of blood and horror. And he had added a rape scene he considered obligatory to any Broadway success. If Langston had fought against any changes, there would have been a legal mess and probably no production. Up to this time only half a dozen black dramatists had been produced on Broadway, and none with any great success. He was undoubtedly very eager to see a Broadway curtain rise on a play of his own. Besides, despite all the changes that had turned *Mulatto* into a melodrama, he felt that the basic meaning of the play—its exposure of racial injustice—was still there.

While race prejudice was indicted on the stage, behind the scenes the producer behaved as though theater was one thing, and life something else. To his opening-night party on Park Avenue, only the white actors in the cast were invited. The Negroes were not asked to come, nor was the author. Even seating in the theater was Jim Crow, with Negroes discouraged from buying seats in the orchestra, until Langston protested and the policy was changed.

The critics, judging the play only by what they saw of Martin Jones's version on the stage, of course, pointed out its weak, muddled structure. But, as Brooks Atkinson of *The New York Times* said, Langston Hughes was "writing about the theme that lies closest to his heart." And in a season dedicated chiefly to trash, the critic welcomed "a playwright who is flaming with sincerity."

Mulatto ran for a year on Broadway, and then it went on the road for two seasons. It established a performance record for a play written by a Negro, a record that stood for twenty-four years, until the young Lorraine Hansberry came along with *Raisin in the Sun*. After World War II *Mulatto* was produced in Argentina, Brazil, Japan, and Italy, where it ran for two years. In 1964, when James Baldwin's play *Blues for Mister Charlie* was presented on Broadway, critics noted the interesting resemblance between Richard Henry, its hero, and Robert Lewis, the hero of Langston's play, written thirty-five years earlier.

18   *Rehearsal*

For most of the next year Langston made Cleveland his home. His ailing mother had moved back there from Oberlin to be near a Negro physician who gave her good care without charging high fees. It was a hard year for Langston. The income from his writing amounted to little. *Mulatto* was playing on the road, but the management was always cutting his royalties or holding them up. When he did collect, it was not enough to make ends meet. There was his mother to support, and he was paying his brother's college tuition at Wilberforce.

But Karamu and the Jelliffes were here, and their theater company was always looking for good material to produce. Years earlier, Charles Gilpin, the actor who had starred in Eugene O'Neill's *Emperor Jones,* had urged Karamu to become a real

Negro theater, to transform the life of its community into drama. Himself criticized for playing the O'Neill role, the unhappy actor had been desperate for honest plays about Negro life that he could give his heart to.

The Karamu people, renaming their company the Gilpin Players, tried to write such plays themselves and, when little came of that, scoured the country for plays on Negro themes.

It was hard to find them. In all its history the Broadway theater had produced only seven plays by Negro writers, with *Mulatto* the latest. The middle-class little-theater groups which had developed in the twenties served up only warmed-over Broadway fare. The Negro college theaters, too, were timid in their choice of plays, relying mostly on Shakespeare, the Greek classics, or Oscar Wilde. No serious black theater could develop without black playwrights. Yet where was the black writer to find the theater that would produce his work?

A radical New Theater movement, born out of the depression, was encouraging Negro writers. Its chief voice and organizing force, *New Theater* magazine, had just run a national prize contest for the best play on a Negro theme. It had counted on the results to supply the demand of its local theater groups for plays on Negro life. In February 1936 the editors announced that a play by Langston Hughes, *Angelo Herndon Jones,* had won the prize, but lamented that not a single other play submitted was worthy of production. And even Langston's play, the editors said, despite significant material and moving scenes, was dramatically weak.

His coming back to Cleveland, both he and Karamu hoped, might prove to be a double blessing. He wanted to write plays and they were eager to put them on. In 1936–37 Karamu staged half a dozen of his works.

One of them was *Drums of Haiti,* the play about Dessalines that had grown out of Langston's trip to the Caribbean island. In New York he had submitted it to most of the Broadway managers, but without success. Some had said they liked it, but in depression times it was too expensive to costume and produce. Others said only Paul Robeson could play the leading role, but he was off in England. Most of the producers were simply not interested in Negro themes.

But Karamu was interested. The way they worked together on a play would begin with Langston drafting a scene and turning it over to the director. As the actors walked through it, trying out the lines and the action, he would see what was clumsy and what worked, what had life in it and what was dead. Then he would go back to his room and work it over again. After a while, he got to know the Gilpin Players and each one's peculiarities, his strengths and his weaknesses. On the stage he could see what each actor's unique personality and talent added to a role, how it intensified or enlarged what his script had sketched in. Soon he began writing parts with particular actors in mind, taking advantage of qualities they could bring to the role. It was the ideal situation theater companies and playwrights rarely find.

But the effect of his productions on the Cleveland community was not always happy. When he wrote plays about contemporary life, some Negroes resented it. *Joy to My Soul* and *Little Ham,* the Jelliffes said, came right out of a raffish local hotel, the Majestic. Langston knew the people in its rooms and lobby and wrote them down sharply, often humorously, but always honestly. Still, there were many who didn't like it. "That represents everything I want to forget," they would say. They did not care to see ghetto life on the stage. If they had climbed into the middle class, they hated to be reminded of where they had come from. Some said whites might believe from these plays that Negroes were content with their segregated lives. Others charged Langston was providing amusement for whites at the expense of Negroes.

It was the old argument of the 1920s, an argument that would rise again twenty years later when church elders would refuse to permit *Simply Heavenly* to be staged in their theater because its action took place in a corner bar and the characters were hardly proper. Why, his critics asked, didn't Negro writers put forward the best racial foot for the world at large to see? "But somewhere back of this misunderstanding," the Jelliffes said, was Langston's "deep conviction that either foot is very good indeed and that all art should be used to reveal life, to hunt out its truths about all men, humble as well as great, rather than to conceal it with superficial drapings."

His own comment on his choice of subjects is implied in his poem, "Litany"—

> Gather up
> In the arms of your love
> Those who expect
> No love from above.

For Langston, writing for the theater was both agonizing work and a lot of fun. Much of the fun came from mixing with the highly volatile people of the theater world. Most of his theater pieces were produced at Karamu, and in later years many would be staged in theaters of all kinds and all over the world. He always thought of himself as first a poet and a writer of books, but he could never stay away from the stage for long. Yet each time he wrote for it, he swore he never would again. Publishing a book, he said, was much simpler than having a play produced.

Producers always had changes to suggest, and when a director got at the play he had changes, too, often the opposite of the revisions the producer demanded. Langston would make all the changes he could without hurting the sense of the play. Then with casting would come another conflict. The director's ideas about the best actor for a part were often opposed to his own. In rehearsals, some scenes would not play well, and had to be revised. Or dropped. Or shifted from the middle of Act Three to the end of Act One. Or new scenes hurriedly written for last-minute insertion. The cutting, shifting, changing, dropping, adding sometimes made the end result so different from the original that Langston could hardly recognize it. He felt lucky if the play the audience saw was at least a fourth of what he had started with.

After some ten plays of his had been produced, he said, "I have learned to trust in the Lord and leave most of the preparatory struggles to the director." He would stay away from rehearsals and come in only a few days before the opening. Then he would sit in the back of the empty theater, watching from the dark the big battles on stage. "Final rehearsals," he said once, "often make better shows than the shows themselves. Such spitting and cussing, such walking and stalking, fainting and crying! All of this is enough to make a writer lose faith in show business." He complained—but he enjoyed the scraps. Once, when he had to leave a rehearsal to do some rewriting at a nearby hotel, he posted a friend in the theater to phone him in case a beautiful row should break out. He hated to miss a display of temperamental fireworks.

His picture of theater work is typical of what most playwrights experience. But some of the difficulties were of his own making. For one thing, he was not a finished craftsman and not a first-rank playwright.

He could create delightful characters and dialogue, and work up some effective scenes, but he could not sustain a large-scale work. He would hammer at a scene or act and then drop it to take up something else. Once, when he had gotten Karamu excited about an idea for a play, and they eagerly agreed to produce it, he sent them a first act from New York. They began rehearsing it at once, expecting the other acts to follow swiftly. But time passed and nothing came. Then, after much long-distance phoning, a second act showed up. They rehearsed this, too, but became panicky when opening date drew near and still no third act. Finally, in desperation, they wrote a third act themselves. Langston showed up in Cleveland for the opening night. After he had seen the performance, he laughed and told the director, "That's just the way I would have finished it!"

As with his poems, he could not be objective or critical about his plays. Perhaps he knew how erratic his judgment was, for producers and directors have remarked on how easy he was to get along with. He did not fight for his lines or scenes as though he were convinced they were the best. Part of this may have been his old difficulty in meeting opposition head on. He would get so upset over a face-to-face clash that he would come down with a sudden cold or bellyache, or simply disappear for a while.

Although he let others revise his theater pieces, he did not hesitate to give them credit if the results were good. After his gospel show, *The Prodigal Son,* began rehearsals in New York, he had to leave for Europe. When he saw it on his return, he wrote in his newspaper column that he was amazed at its success, because when he left New York the show was "a shambles." He paid tribute to Vinette Carroll and Syvilla Fort, the director and the choreographer, for changing it from a speech-song play to a swinging dance pantomime, in the course of which they took out almost all of his lines. "In the process it had become a novel concoction I never dreamed of, but a delightful one," he wrote. "And its moral has not been lost. My faith in show business is restored."

19 The Bloody Spanish Earth

In the late spring of 1937 the Baltimore *Afro-American* asked Langston to go to Spain as their war correspondent. They wanted him to report on the American Negroes fighting in the International Brigade. He knew Spanish, of course, from his long stays in Mexico. Spain he knew only slightly: his ship had touched a port or two on his way back from Europe twelve years ago. He had long wanted to go back and stay. Now that the chance had come, he was not sure. Seeing Spain tourist style was one thing. But in the midst of a savage civil war?

Like many Americans, Langston was deeply moved by the passionate resistance of the Spanish people to Franco. The war had begun in July 1936, when most of Spain's army officers revolted against the Republican government. They were confident that they could capture power in a few days and set up a dictatorship.

But the revolt turned into a civil war. The mass of the common soldiers and the common people refused to surrender. The war became a bloody, savage conflict between the privileged and the deprived. To most of the outside world it was at once seen as a war between democracy, represented by the elected government, and the fascists, or those who sought to destroy democracy, represented by General Franco and the military forces of Hitler and Mussolini, who came swiftly to his aid.

An underground railroad was already running from California across all the states, picking up hundreds of American volunteers and carrying them to the French-Spanish border, where they moved up into battle. Each one of them had gone out of a mixture of feelings and motives, some political, some personal. For Langston it was like that, too. He hated what Franco stood for, he wanted his pen to rally support for the antifascist fighters, he wanted to test his own courage under fire. But he also wanted to get out from under a mountain of cares— the scratching, grinding necessity of making ends meet, the painful burden of his mother's fatal illness (she would die in 1938), his unhappiness in Cleveland. He must have been thinking of other escape routes, for that April *Opportunity* advertised a sixty-day tour of the Soviet Union, to study the art and folkways of its minority racial groups, a tour to be led by Langston Hughes. Before anything could come of it, he was offered the chance to go to Spain for perhaps half a year, with income guaranteed. He took it.

He came to New York and, with the advice of his old friend and lawyer, Arthur Spingarn, made out his will. (There was little to leave anyone— only the hope of future royalties.)

He paid his mother's rent for three months ahead, and arranged for his *Mulatto* royalties to be banked for her. In July he reached Paris. There he teamed up with Nicolás Guillén, the Cuban poet, who was also going to Spain as a reporter. The day they boarded the train for Barcelona the Paris papers headlined that German and Italian planes had just bombed the port city and killed several hundred people.

Barcelona was lit only by stars when they arrived. The buildings towered dark in the night, with windows shuttered and shades drawn, and no lights visible to guide enemy bombers. They walked the streets awhile, to watch the crowds strolling in the warm air and listening to the war news blaring from radios in cafes. It was long after midnight before Langston fell asleep in his hotel room on the Ramblas.

His sleep was shattered by a terrific explosion that flung him out of his bed. He staggered down to the lobby to join the other guests huddled in their pajamas. He trembled violently at the sound of a major battle going on outside the windows. But it was only the antiaircraft guns firing at enemy planes. His fright gave him the worst bellyache he had ever suffered. Soon the firing died away, and everyone went back to bed.

Barcelona and Madrid were the first European cities to be bombed from the air on a big scale. It was a new and filthy page in history. Death fell out of the sky on all alike—soldiers or civilians. Without air defenses the Spanish cities lay helpless. In the first month in Madrid a thousand were killed, three thousand injured, and a third of the city was leveled.

As the days and weeks passed, Langston got used

to air raids and the sounds of bombs falling. These were German and Italian planes overhead; Franco's side never lacked for such help. Hitler and Mussolini poured in planes, tanks, pilots, technicians, troops. But the democratic powers, Britain and France and the United States, decided not to intervene, and denied arms to the legal government in violation of its international rights and all historical practice. The Russians sent limited help to the Loyalists—oil, food, arms, technical and military advisors. But every appeal of the Spanish government to the League of Nations for the right to buy arms in its own defense was turned down.

Denied the help of governments, the Loyalists found that their cause drew overwhelming moral support of the people everywhere—workers, writers, artists, intellectuals. Men stole across the French frontier into Spain from all over the world, to fight in what they believed was a just cause—the defense of democracy against fascism. Some forty thousand men came as volunteers for the International Brigade, though there were never more than eighteen thousand in Spain at any one time. And many others came to serve as doctors, nurses, and technicians.

On a much bigger scale it was like the war in

Greece a hundred years earlier, when Americans like Samuel Gridley Howe and Englishmen like Lord Byron went to help Greece win its independence from the Turks.

For six months Langston was close to the battlefields of Spain, living in the cities under constant bombing attack, and going up to the front lines, where he talked to scores of Negroes who had volunteered in the American battalions. These were named after Lincoln, Washington, and John Brown, with one of the machine-gun companies named after Frederick Douglass. He found men from St. Louis and Pittsburgh, Boston and Buffalo, New York and Los Angeles, Cleveland and San Francisco, from almost everywhere back home, it seemed.

Langston found that the International Brigade was integrated. Negroes and whites served in mixed companies, with Negro officers having white soldiers under their command, too. There were many Negroes in the medical units. Two of the ambulance drivers were colored teen-agers who had somehow escaped from high school to come here and drive up to the fronts under fire and bring back the wounded. One of the surgeons was Dr. Arnold Donawa of Harlem, a tall, kindly man in charge of rebuilding the faces of wounded soldiers. One of his nurses was Salaria Kee, a slender young Negro woman from Akron, Ohio.

Once, while visiting on the Ebro front, Langston was asked to read some of his poems for a group of the Brigaders resting on the cold stone floor of an old mill. He had been writing about the war while he was on the scene, calling the verses *Letters from Spain.* One of his poems was "Tomorrow's Seed":

> Proud banners of death,
> I see them waving
> There against the sky,
> Struck deep in Spanish earth
> Where your dark bodies lie
> Inert and helpless—
> So they think
> Who do not know
> That from your death
> New life will grow.
> For there are those who cannot see
> The mighty roots of liberty
> Push upward in the dark
> To burst in flame—
> A million stars—

And one your name:
  Man
Who fell in Spanish earth:
Human seed
  For freedom's birth.

After the reading, the soldiers talked about the poems, their comments interrupted by the roar of artillery. Why do you sometimes use incorrect grammar and slightly broken English? a soldier wanted to know. Many of our Negro Brigaders are well educated. Besides, won't this help make stronger the stereotype of the illiterate Negro?

Langston answered that of course most of the Negroes in the Brigade spoke grammatically, but that others—and lots of whites, too—didn't, because they had had little formal education. Negroes from states like Georgia, Alabama, and Mississippi had gone to very poor schools at best. And one of the things Langston was trying to do in these poems was to show that even Americans denied their own rights were fighting to help Spanish workers and farmers preserve a government that would give everybody an equal chance at schooling.

In Madrid, under siege by Franco's forces, Langston was asked to stay at the Alianza, a beautiful fifty-room mansion made into a clubhouse for Spanish writers and artists. It had been the home of a rebel marquis whose family fortune came down from slave trading on the Spanish Main. There was a fine view of Madrid; at night you could see the enemy guns flashing as they poured shells into the city. Breakfast at the Alianza was a single roll and coffee. Dinner was a concoction of whatever scraps of food the cook could find.

During night bombardments, everyone living in the Alianza would gather in the same room to listen to music. When Langston arrived with his records they enjoyed drowning out Franco's shells with Duke Ellington and Benny Goodman. The city had been living under fire for a year. Now the people had gotten over their terror. Bombs falling were treated like showers falling—simply something to duck out of. Front-line trenches came right into the city. But in the streets Langston saw children (there were 100,000 still here) playing hide-and-seek in the shell holes. "The will to live and laugh in this city of over a million people under fire, each person in constant danger, was to me a source of amazement. One could forget the possibility of imminent death, but it was impossible not to be cold as winter came, or always half-hungry."

For Langston there was always the knowledge that he, an American, could leave whenever he liked. But the Spaniards had no choice. He wondered how long they could resist like this. There were no signs of surrender in Madrid. And no heroics about it— no speeches or bands or parades. The longer he stayed in Madrid, the more he liked it. The people were hungry—but they still had hope.

At the Alianza the poets, the musicians, the artists, the actors, used their talents to help fight the war. They did not want to live in a Franco Spain in which the books they wrote would be censored or burned. They placed their art at the service of the Republic. They painted posters, wrote books and poems and songs and plays. Actors who fought in the nearby trenches came in to perform in the theaters. Most of the men in the Alianza were soldiers, too, who worked at their art when they were on leave.

In December Langston knew it was time to go. He had already stayed long beyond the time the newspaper had asked. And he had seen almost everything and written all the stories he could find. With less and less food, he was eating into supplies the Spaniards needed. Potato peelings and sausage skins were being boiled to make soup. Horsemeat was now a luxury. It was said that people were even eating their cats.

At five one morning Langston took the bus for Valencia. Madrid seemed deserted except for the military patrols. As the bus lurched through the dusky streets a deep sadness came over him. He hated to leave the city he had come to love. He felt sick in his stomach and in his soul all the long way to Valencia. It took a week to get a seat on a train going north to the French border. Then he was through the Pyrenees and in a French village on the other side—beyond the noise of shells and bombs for the first time in six months.

Yet less than a mile away was Spain. "What a difference a border makes," he thought. "On one side of an invisible line, food; on the other side, none. On one side, peace; on the other side, war. On one side, quiet in the sunlight; on the other side the dangerous chee-eep, chee-eep, chee-eep that was not birds, the BANG! of shells, the whine of sirens, and the bursting of bombs over crowded cities. I stood alone on the platform that bright December day and looked down the valley into Spain and wondered about borders and nationalities and war. I wondered what would happen to the Spanish people walking the bloody tightrope of their civil struggle."

He did not know it then, but the Spanish people were falling off the tightrope, falling off the wrong way. Franco was winning. In 1939 it would be over. Of the 3200 Americans who came to fight in Spain, 1800 were killed, and most of the survivors were wounded at least once.

It was Christmas when Langston reached Paris. He stayed at an Ethiopian hotel, the only "colored" one in town, not because he had to, but because to him it was fun. It was full of Ethiopians, Sudanese, Algerians coming and going. From its windows he could see Montmartre. During the holidays he met many old friends—Jacques Roumains of Haiti, Henri Cartier-Bresson and his wife, and his French publisher, Pierre Seghers.

They all talked of war, not only of the war in Spain but of a war everyone was sure would come, a war they feared would engulf Europe and perhaps the world. The Parisians said Spain was a training ground for Hitler and Mussolini. When their bombers and troops were ready, they would spread the war everywhere. Many of the Americans living in Paris were thinking of going home. Langston had hoped to spend the winter in Paris, but he couldn't afford it.

New Year's Eve found him walking the cold boulevards. He had gone alone to the opera. Now, as he was returning to his room, the snow began to sift slowly over the rooftops. The streets were very quiet and lonely. He wondered where everybody could be as Paris moved into the first hours of the New Year.

He thought back over the last five years since he had decided to be a professional writer. His work had earned him a living, and it had taken him to so many places—Mexico City, Carmel, Moscow, Tashkent, New York, Madrid, Paris. No matter where he was, he found work he wanted to do. And he had been able to keep his promise to himself—to write only what he wanted to write. He knew his range had broadened, too. Not only the American Negro, but colored people—all people—everywhere concerned him now.

20 *Theater in a Suitcase*

It was January 1938 when Langston got back to New York to take up the job of building a Negro theater in the middle of Harlem. He wanted to see a theater that would sink its roots deep into Negro life, a theater that would present plays by black writers, with black actors and directors and scenic designers learning to master all the necessary crafts. It would be a theater that would voice the moods and thoughts of black people, finding the shape and rhythm of the life being lived in the sprawling miles of Harlem's streets and tenements.

Working with others, he set about making a theater out of a loft on the second story of an old building on West 125th Street. They called it the Harlem Suitcase Theater because all the equipment

they had could have been squeezed into one suitcase. Their aim, they said, was "to present plays of
Negro life applying especially to the Harlem community at prices no higher than neighborhood
movies, with community actors, and with all profits
returned to a sinking fund."

The first production was Langston's *Don't You
Want To Be Free?* It was billed as "a poetry play,
from slavery through the blues to now—and then
some!" He used about a dozen of his poems for it,
writing dramatic sketches that built up to them. Into
the action he wove spirituals, blues, work chants,
and jazz. His goal was to entertain the audience
and, at the same time, to educate it. He staged it
with no scenery or curtains, and put the action right
in the center of the theater, with the audience seated
all around it. For it he borrowed many experimental
techniques he had admired in Russian theaters during his long stay there. It was probably New York's
first arena theater, or theater-in-the-round, a new
form widely adopted in later years.

Don't You Want To Be Free? opened on April
21, 1938. Tickets were thirty-five cents and performances were given on weekends only, when
working people could come. After a while the play

was moved into the basement of Harlem's Countee Cullen Branch Library. One hundred and thirty-five performances were given, the longest consecutive run ever recorded in Harlem.

That year the country was seized again by the despairing mood of the earlier thirties. For a time the New Deal's pump-priming had seemed to work, but now business had slumped badly again. No matter what the government improvised to ease the shock, it was never enough to lift the nation into prosperity. And again, by every measure—their share of relief, of jobs, of wages, of low-cost housing —Negroes were worse off than whites. Many Harlem families had been driven literally underground. Over ten thousand Negroes lived in cellars and basements, along with the rats. They huddled together in the damp concrete dungeons with a barred slit for a window and a tin can for a toilet.

Reacting to the prolonged crisis, some of what Langston wrote now had little chance to endure. He was often too caught up in the day-to-day battles to be able to do more than pamphleteer. If his writing could help organize people to protest their suffering, he would do it. He wrote more poems about the Scottsboro boys, still in prison in Alabama, about Tom Mooney, the labor organizer imprisoned in California, poems about blacks on the plantation and in the ghetto, about lynchings and Spain and unions and freedom and equality. He spoke not only for "the Negro bearing slavery's scars," as in his long poem "Let America Be America Again," but for the poor whites cheated and lied to, the red man driven from the land, the immigrant on relief. Would America ever be the dream the dreamers dreamed?

Many of the poems of this period were printed in a cheap booklet called *A New Song,* in the hope that they would reach large numbers of working people for the first time. That year, too, Langston teamed with the pianist-composer James P. Johnson, to write a short blues opera, *The Organizer,* which could be simply staged anywhere. It was based on the underground struggle in the South to build a union of sharecroppers.

Still doing all he could to aid the Spanish Loyalists, Langston translated and published their poet, García Lorca, whom the fascists had murdered. When the International Congress of Writers for the Defense of Culture was held in Paris in July, Langston and the novelist Theodore Dreiser were sent as delegates from America.

Early in 1939, with the Suitcase Theater beginning to work on other productions, he went west to found the New Negro Theater in Los Angeles. It began its first season with *Don't You Want To Be Free?* (The play was even reaching into the South, where a community theater in Nashville had staged it.) As usual, Langston was soon juggling a dozen balls in the air. He was working on memoirs of his childhood and youth, scheduled for publication by Knopf. In March, returning some money he had borrowed from a friend, he wrote, "The movies have got me at long last, and although they seem a far cry from Art with a big A, they at least help a person to pay his debts." The film was a vehicle for the child singing star Bobby Breen. Called *Way Down South,* it had a pre-Civil War background. Langston wrote the screenplay with Clarence Muse, a veteran Negro actor who had appeared in many movies, and the lyrics for music to be sung by the Hall Johnson Choir. It is still one of the rare films for which Hollywood hired Negro writers.

In May he left Hollywood, the movie money in his hand, and holed up in the Hotel Grand in Chicago to finish his autobiography. In September, broke again, he was back in Carmel, asking and getting from Knopf a small loan against the delivery of the manuscript. He mailed it to New York in

November, telling his editor that after the winter lecture tour he planned to start on a second novel. Every year or two he would mention the novel, always hoping to earn enough money to buy the time to write it. He never did.

The autobiography, taking Langston up to the age of twenty-eight, appeared in the fall of 1940 as *The Big Sea*. It was welcomed by the critics as a warm and entertaining portrait of the early years of a Negro writer. Richard Wright, whose first novel, *Native Son,* came out that year, reviewed *The Big Sea*. He paid tribute to Langston for his major role in creating a realistic literature of the Negro, and in acting as a "cultural ambassador," representing through his writing the Negro's case at the court of world opinion. He liked the book for its humor and objectivity. "Hughes is tough," he said; "he bends but he never breaks." He thought Langston had developed "a range of artistic interest and expression possessed by no other Negro writer of his time."

Another most significant review was written by a young Negro critic who a dozen years later would reach a high rank in American literature with his novel *The Invisible Man*. Ralph Ellison saw *The Big Sea* as an evocative and valuable record of the

Negro Renaissance by "one of the few writers who survived [it] and still has the vitality to create." The book had all the excitement of a picaresque novel, he said. His one regret, and an important one, was that Langston had not given the reader enough analysis and comment. Next time he hoped Hughes would show "the processes by which a sensitive Negro attains a heightened consciousness of a world in which most of the odds are against his doing so."

Whether in response to that comment or not, Langston was thinking about the forces that shaped the black consciousness. The written word is the most important record we have of our present lives and our past to leave behind for future generations.

Suppose *Native Son*'s Bigger Thomas (excellently drawn as he is) was the sole survivor on the bookshelves of tomorrow [he asked]. Or my own play, *Mulatto,* whose end consists of murder, madness and suicide? If the best of our writers continue to pour their talent into the tragedies of frustration and weakness, tomorrow will probably say, on the basis of available literary evidence, "No wonder the Negroes never amounted to anything. There were no heroes among them. Defeat and panic, moaning, groaning, and weeping were their lot. Did nobody fight? Did nobody triumph?"

Where, he asked, is that great creative series of biographies and novels and plays about Harriet Tubman, Sojourner Truth, Frederick Douglass, Nat Turner? The field of humor has been explored, although mostly by white writers, and so have the fields of frustration and tragedy, of folklore, of the practical progress of the race. "But where, in all these books, is that compelling flame of spirit and passion that makes a man say, 'I, too, am a hero, because my race has produced heroes like that?' "

He thought words had been used too often to make people doubt and fear. "Words should be used to make people *believe* and *do*," he said. Writers have power, he believed, and are responsible for the way they use it. Surely that power should not make people believe in the wrong things—in death instead of life, in suffering instead of joy, in oppression instead of freedom.

Believing in the need for heroes, Langston himself had to do something about it. He applied for and was granted a Rosenwald fellowship to write historical plays suitable for use in Negro schools and colleges. Then he went to work near Monterey at

Noel Sullivan's Hollow Hills Farm. He tried his hand at historical drama and found time too for many of the short stories that later appeared in his collection *Laughing to Keep from Crying,* and several of the poems that would go into the book *Shakespeare in Harlem.*

Richard Wright once said of Langston that he made ceaseless movement one of his life principles. "Six months in one place," he told Wright, "is long enough to make one's life complicated." So again, in late 1941, he turned east and started another theater (his third), this time in Chicago. The Skyloft Players were based in the Good Shepherd Community House. It began to look as though whenever he wanted a play produced, he started another group. For he had brought with him his new historical play with music, *The Sun Do Move.* The title came from the famous sermon given countless times in the slave South by the legendary Negro preacher John Jasper of Richmond. The theme was the Underground Railroad.

The New York and Los Angeles companies died after a time, but the Chicago group is still in existence. Short-lived or not, these early Negro companies were the forerunners of many little-theater groups that sprang up in Negro communities throughout the country. They encouraged young Negroes to write for the stage. The only way they could learn was by seeing their work performed, and there were few other places a black writer could turn to. Out of the companies came many actors who won professional standing.

In the summer of 1942 Langston came back to Harlem. He moved into a three-room apartment at 634 St. Nicholas Avenue, sharing it with two old friends of his family from Kansas days, Emerson and Toy Harper. They were like adopted uncle and aunt to him. Mr. Harper, a musician who had played in Fletcher Henderson's band, was also a composer who wrote songs with Langston. Aunt Toy was a dress designer. She had done the costumes for *Don't You Want To Be Free?* and had also acted in the cast.

The war begun by Hitler had now engulfed the world. The Japanese, allied to the Nazis, had attacked Pearl Harbor in December 1941, bringing America into the war. Langston, who had been too young to fight in World War I, was too old to fight in World War II. But he wanted to do all he could to help defeat Hitler's racists.

Nevertheless, supporting the United States government in this war was not an easy decision for many Negroes to make. For at home there was racism, too, racism American style. Its signs were all about. The war production plants clamored for labor, but turned Negroes away. The armed forces looked for manpower, but used quotas to keep Negroes out, or gave them only menial tasks.

Under the leadership of A. Philip Randolph, head of the Brotherhood of Sleeping Car Porters, Negroes organized a March on Washington movement that forced President Roosevelt to issue an executive order barring Jim Crow in defense industries and in government employment.

There was still discrimination in the Army, Navy and Air Corps. But Negroes were determined to end it. They were finding out that they got more when they yelled than when they pleaded. If Hitler won, there would be no chance for the survivors to fight oppression anywhere. So Langston put his talent at the service of the war against fascism. He wrote verses and slogans for the Treasury Department to help sell defense bonds. And for the Writers War Board he produced articles to tell the country what Negroes were doing in all the branches of service.

He teamed up with such composers as W. C.

Handy, Clarence Jones, and Elie Siegmeister, writing the lyrics for songs the soldiers were soon singing. Some of his work was broadcast on the radio networks or presented at freedom rallies in places like Madison Square Garden. Later Langston got special satisfaction from learning that the Dutch underground movement had secretly published some of his writing in a booklet called *Lament for Dark Peoples and Other Poems*. They circulated it as a weapon against the Nazis occupying their country.

In 1942 came Langston's first major collection of poems in fifteen years, *Shakespeare in Harlem*. He called it "a book of light verse, Afro Americana in the blues mood." He probably meant "light verse" in the sense that the forms were simple blues, ballads, and reels. For the themes were hardly light— loneliness, hunger, death in Harlem, on the South Side, on Beale Street. The sixty-odd poems were meant to be read aloud, crooned, shouted, recited, and sung, he said. And so they have been, for several adaptations of them have been made for radio, television, and the stage.

Yearly he continued to go on his poetry reading tours, sometimes appearing in as many as seventeen states during a season. In 1944 he spoke at many high schools, using his poems to help instill race pride in Negro students and to interpret Negro life to white students. Many of the schools Langston visited had never presented Negro speakers in the assemblies. He talked to the boys and girls about black history, about the heroism of Negro soldiers and sailors and airmen, about the problems that beset a wartime democracy.

"White folks fear colored folks," he said. "England fears America, both fear Russia. The Nordics fear the Orientals, and the Orientals fear the Nordics. Africa knows that civilization is still making a grab bag out of the Dark Continent.

"Of course, this war may change things for the better. People all over the world may wake up and stop trying to exploit each other. It takes a very hard kick in the pants, however, to wake the average human being up to the point of doing anything very widely constructive in a social way. But since large portions of the human race are busy at this moment kicking other portions in the pants with shot and shell, bomb and submarine, perhaps it will help.

"Maybe," he said, "maybe this war will jar some decency into all of us, thus making the world to come a better world."

21

Poems—
and Politics

"Poets who write mostly about love, roses and moonlight, sunsets and snow," Langston said once, "must lead a very quiet life. Seldom, I imagine, does their poetry get them into difficulties."

He rarely wrote about love as something way off in the blue. His love was love in a very particular place, Harlem, usually, where people had problems. Even many of his earliest poems could be called social poems in that they were about common problems, rather than his personal troubles alone. Often, of course, some aspects of his private difficulties happened to be the same as others'. And racially, his own desire to realize the dream of American life—"land where opportunity is real, life is free, and equality is the air we breathe"—was the same as that of millions of other segregated blacks.

His poems, he found out early, could get him into

trouble. The first time it happened was in a colored church in Atlanta, just after *The Weary Blues* had been published. He was reading from some of his blues poems about hard luck and hard work. In the middle, a deacon approached the pulpit and put a note beside Langston. He didn't stop to read it until he had finished and the applause had ended. The note read, "Do not read any more blues in my pulpit." It was signed by the minister.

During the 1920s he was forbidden to visit Cuba by the Machado dictatorship because he had written some poems about the way the sugar plantation owners exploited the cane workers. But it was not until he had been to Soviet Russia that censorship got bad enough to keep him many times from appearing on public programs. It started when he was scheduled to be one of several speakers at a program in the colored YMCA branch in Los Angeles. Some people charged he was a communist and the scared Y secretary said that unless Langston was dropped the program couldn't go on. Langston had never been a communist but he soon learned it didn't make any difference to the people making the charge. Anyone visiting Russia in those days and reporting anything favorable to it was liable to have the label slapped on him. Even Eleanor Roosevelt, the President's wife, and people like Walter White of the NAACP, and Mrs. Bethune were called "red." The voices who cried "red" the loudest, Langston noted dryly, were never known to be raised against segregation. The groups that opposed his poetry readings, he saw time and again, were the same ones who did not wish Negroes to vote, achieve equality in education, or be given a square deal in jobs or housing.

It amounted to this: If you said or wrote anything about the American dream falling short of its promise, if you pointed out weaknesses in our society, if you criticized the way things were, there were people who would attack you immediately as a radical, a leftist, or a communist. They would not tolerate protest. It was easier to try to shut a critic's mouth than to answer his argument. They never heard, or would rather forget, Jefferson's words: "Error of opinion may be tolerated where reason is left free to combat it."

In spite of the Y secretary's ruling, the youth committee refused to give in to pressure. But the police were put at the door to keep Langston out that Sunday afternoon. The young people then told the assembled audience what was happening, and moved the meeting to another place where Langston was allowed to speak.

A near riot broke out in November 1940 when he was to read a few poems with several other authors at a Book and Author luncheon in a Pasadena hotel. Somebody malicious gave Aimee Semple McPherson, the highly publicized evangelist, a copy of Langston's youthful poem "Goodbye Christ." It was ironic in tone and meant to be a poem against those he felt were misusing religion for profit. In it he mentioned Miss McPherson. She was furious, and claimed the poem was anti-Christian. From her pulpit she preached against Langston, saying, "There are many devils, but the most dangerous of all is the red devil. And now there comes among us a red devil *in a black skin!*"

Her followers showed up to picket the hotel the afternoon he was to speak. They sent a delegation into the hotel "to interrogate me," he said, "on the state of my immortal soul." As their sound truck blared out "God Bless America" the howling mob blocked all traffic. The frantic hotel manager said Langston would have to leave or he would cancel the entire luncheon. Rather than inconvenience the several hundred guests already there and the half-dozen other speakers, Langston withdrew, barely getting through the mob as the police cars came up in answer to a riot call.

"Later," he said, "I learned from the afternoon papers that the whole demonstration had been organized by Aimee McPherson's publicity man, and that when the police arrived he had been arrested for refusing to give up the keys to his sound truck stalled midway the street to block traffic. This simply proved the point I had tried to make in the poem —that the church might as well bid Christ goodbye if his gospel were left in the hands of such people."

A few years later Langston was picketed again, this time in Detroit by the "Mothers of America," a group organized by Gerald L. K. Smith. Smith was the man who fomented a riot in Detroit's Sojourner Truth housing project in the hope of keeping Negroes out of the government homes built for them.

To be picketed—and it would continue to happen every now and then—was never pleasant, but at least he felt he must be saying something worth while. He wasn't turning his back on his people's problems or his country's. Nothing like this would happen to him if he limited the subjects of his poems to roses and moonlight. But almost all the beautiful roses he had seen were in white people's yards, not in his.

Once in Gary, Indiana, the colored teachers were threatened with the loss of their jobs if Langston accepted their invitation to speak at one of the public schools. In another city a white high school principal, hounded by a few reactionary parents, sought assurance from the FBI, who seemingly told him the scheduled speaker was not a communist. But the principal of the white school still needed to bolster his respectability. When Langston showed up for the assembly he found that all the Negro ministers and other black notables in town had been invited to sit on the stage in a semicircle behind him. Stepping out to read his poems, he felt like Mr. Interlocutor in a modern minstrel show. The students must have been overwhelmed, he thought, by this sudden wave of blackness after all those years when they had never seen any Negroes at all on their stage.

Coming back home once after completing forty-five speaking dates, he wrote, "It's been a running feud with Klan-minded censors from Florida to California who like neither poetry nor Negroes." And so it went into the 1950s. There was no telling

238

when a wave of know-nothing patriotism might seize a community or the whole nation. In 1951 even the venerable Dr. Du Bois was threatened with jail by the federal government. Langston came to the defense of his childhood hero in a syndicated newspaper column written in words of fire. At the end he said:

Somebody in Washington wants to put Dr. Du Bois in jail. Somebody in France wanted to put Voltaire in jail. Somebody in Franco's Spain sent Lorca, their greatest poet, to death before a firing squad. Somebody in Germany under Hitler burned the books, drove Thomas Mann into exile, and led their leading Jewish scholars to the gas chamber. Somebody in Greece long ago gave Socrates the hemlock to drink. Somebody at Golgotha erected a cross and somebody drove the nails into the hands of Christ. Somebody spat upon his garments. No one remembers their names.

Thousands of men and women were victimized in those years for their dissenting opinions. For a long time, during the years when Senator Joseph McCarthy dominated Washington and the headlines, any writer with an independent mind and the courage to speak it was fair game for state or Congressional investigating committees.

And Langston was among them. He was summoned before the McCarthy committee in March 1953, when the Wisconsin Senator was trying to embarrass a government agency by accusing it of purchasing radical books for distribution to libraries overseas. A few of Langston's early books were on the list. Queried about his political beliefs, he said he had never been a communist, and did not believe in anything but a democratic solution to social and economic problems. Pressed to give the names of people he might know to be communists, he refused to involve anyone else. The committee dismissed him, but that was not the end. The effect upon him, as upon so many others, was serious. His lecturing, an important source of his income, fell off badly for a long time, and even to his last days on the circuit, there were always some to picket his readings or try to stop them.

McCarthy was finally discredited before the nation and censured by his fellow Senators. But there was no guarantee that such hysteria would not come again.

22   *Simple Speaks His Mind*

No one, himself included, realized what would come of it that day in the Harlem bar when Langston met a man called Simple.

It happened this way. One night—it was during World War II—Langston was sitting in a cafe when he saw a young fellow who lived just down the block from him. "Come on over and meet my girl friend," the man said. The three sat down in a booth over beers and, not knowing much about him, Langston asked where he worked. "In a war plant," he said.

"What do you make?"

"Cranks," he answered.

"What kind of cranks?"

"Oh, man, I don't know what kind of cranks."

"Well," asked Langston, "do they crank cars, trucks, buses, planes or what?"

"I don't know what them cranks crank," he said.

At which his girl friend, a little annoyed, put in, "You've been working there long enough. By now you ought to know what them cranks crank."

"Aw woman," he said, "you know white folks don't tell colored folks what cranks crank!"

And that was how "Simple" began. "Out of the mystery as to what the cranks of the world crank, to whom they belong and why," Langston said, he created the character of Simple, "wondering and laughing at the numerous problems of white folks, colored folks, and just folks—including himself." Langston was writing a weekly column for the Negro newspaper, the Chicago *Defender,* and into it he began putting his Simple stories. The first one appeared in 1943, with Simple talking about everything under the sun, from love to lynching, from intermarriage to international affairs.

Simple is not simple at all. That is only his deceptive nickname. Jesse B. Semple is his proper real name. He has little formal education, but a lot of sense, sense taught him by the trials and tribulations of the life he has lived. But let him explain himself:

I have had so many hardships in this life that it is a wonder I'll live until I die. I was born young, black, voteless, poor, and hungry, in a state where white folks did not even put Negroes on the census.

Then he goes on to tell how life is for him, beginning from the bottom up:

These feet of mine have stood in everything from soup lines to the draft board. They have supported everything from a packing trunk to a hungry woman. My feet have walked ten thousand miles running errands for white folks and another ten thousand trying to keep up with colored. My feet have stood before altars, at crap tables, bars, graves, kitchen doors, welfare windows, and social security railings. . . . And from my feet up, so many other things have happened to me, since, it is a wonder I made it through this world. In my time, I have been cut, stabbed, run over, hit by a car, tromped by a horse, robbed, fooled, deceived, double-crossed, dealt seconds, and mighty near blackmailed—but I am still here! I have been laid off, fired and not rehired, jim crowed, segregated, insulted, eliminated, locked in, locked out, locked up, left holding the bag, and denied relief. I have been caught in the rain, caught in jails, caught short with my rent, and caught with the wrong woman—but I am still here!

My mama should have named me Job instead of Jesse B. Semple. I have been underfed, underpaid, undernourished, and everything but undertaken—yet I am still here. The only thing I am afraid of now—is that I will die before my time.

Simple was Langston's own answer to the plea he uttered long ago for an end to stories in which the Negro characters are always completely done in by life. With all his troubles, there is nothing doomed about Simple.

The Simple stories, like Langston's poems, document how the Negro people feel. "If you want to understand the black brother," one Negro critic advised, "learn to know Simple." In the sketches there are usually two characters speaking: Simple, who is an untrained, honest, hard-working Harlemite, up from Virginia, and a well-educated man, a writer, who could be Hughes himself. This character is like a straight man, always arguing with and needling Simple, wanting to think things through, to do the right thing from the liberal point of view. But Simple acts from his real feelings, and if he doesn't like something he says so. There is a balance between the two, a give and take, that keep the scenes in Paddy's Bar rich and funny.

Simple is first and last a "race man." "I have been caught in some kind of riffle ever since I been black," he says. He walks around with the fate of the black brother always on his mind. "No matter what a man does, sick or well, something is always liable to happen, especially if you are colored," he warns.

If Hughes tells him he is tired of his always bringing up the race question, Simple's answer comes fast: He doesn't have to bring it up, it's there. "I look in the mirror in the morning to shave—and what do I see? Me." Around the clock he knows he lives in a color-conscious world.

When Simple appeared in the first book, *Simple Speaks His Mind,* some people asked Langston, "Why write about a man like that, from a place called Harlem? Why not write about more universal characters?" And others even said, "Why write about Negroes at all? Why not just people?"

Which sounded a bit as though they didn't believe Negroes were people. The questions showed that some folks thought very few people could identify with that small part of the world called Harlem. Langston's answer was, "I felt that by writing honestly enough and truthfully enough and beautifully enough about *one* man in *one* place on *one* corner, 125th and Lenox, people around the world might recognize him as being one of them, no matter where they lived."

He proved to be right. Standing on his doorstep, he could reach the world. The five Simple books have been translated into several languages. People in Paris, Amsterdam, Helsinki, Copenhagen, Cape Town, Hamburg, and London read and recognize Simple. He seemed so real and believable to them that a Tennessee reader once sent him a possum packed in ice after Langston had written that Simple liked possum meat.

Those readers are proof of what some critics have said: that Simple is the finest contribution Langston Hughes has made to American literature. They have compared Simple to the comic creations of Mark Twain and Sholem Aleichem.

There were always a few voices, however, that

would ask, "What's so funny about being black? And in white America?"

But Langston pointed out, "Colored people are always laughing at some wry Jim Crow incident or absurd nuance of the color line. If Negroes took all the white world's boorishness to heart and wept over it as profoundly as our serious writers do, we would have been dead long ago."

Besides, he went on:

Humor is a weapon, too, of no mean value against one's foes. In the Latin American countries it is used socially. The humorous magazines there are often more dangerous to a crooked politician than the most serious articles in the intellectual press. . . . The race problem in America is serious business, I admit. But must it *always* be written about seriously? So many weighty volumes, cheerless novels, sad tracts, and violent books have been written on race relations that I would like to see some writers of both races write about our problems with black tongue in white cheek, or vice versa. Sometimes I try. Simple helps me.

But after a quarter century of writing about the character, Langston began to feel he had exhausted Simple. Besides, he told an interviewer, "The racial climate has gotten so complicated and bitter that cheerful and ironic humor is less and less understandable to so many people."

He was not discouraged about the value of humor, however. In 1966 he edited *The Book of Negro Humor,* putting into it jokes, jive, nonsense verses, songs, folk tales, and a dozen other varieties. "Humor is your own unconscious therapy," he said in a prefatory note. "Like a welcome summer rain, humor may suddenly cleanse and cool the earth, the air, and you."

23 I Used to Wonder

I used to wonder
About living and dying—
I think the difference lies
Between tears and crying.

I used to wonder
About here and there—
I think the distance
Is nowhere.

That poem of his, "Border Line," was one of Langston Hughes' favorites. His reasons for liking it so much tell something about poetry itself, as well as about how he wrote it.

" 'Border Line,' " he said, "seems to carry within itself a melody which I can hear although I cannot sing a note. Since this poem is like a song, its sound

conditioned its saying. *What* it says is therefore so
much of a piece with the way it is said that form and
content are one, like a circle whose shape is itself
and whose self is its shape, and which could be no
other way than to be what it is. I did not consciously
compose this poem. It came to me, and I simply
wrote it down, and wondered where it came from,
and liked it. Possibly I like it because it was not
contrived, its inception having been outside myself."

Good writing, he told students, comes out of your
own life. You start at home, with what you know
best—your own family, your neighborhood, your
city. "You will find the whole world just outside
your doorstep even if, seemingly, there is nothing
there but the concrete sidewalk and a water plug.
You will find the world in your own eyes, if they
learn how to see, in your heart if it learns how to
feel, and in your own fingers if they learn how to
touch. What your fingers transfer to paper—if you
are able to make yourself into a writer—will grow
and grow and grow until it reaches everybody's
world."

Much of Hughes' work echoed the mood and
tempo of jazz. Very early there were such poems as
"Jazzonia" and "Negro Dancers," which he showed
to Vachel Lindsay in the Washington hotel. Later,

he experimented with the new be-bop music he heard in Harlem. He worked fragments of conversation into a kind of poetic jam session, with voices taking solos and cutting in on one another, as in his 1951 book, *Montage of a Dream Deferred.*

As the "original jazz poet" (Arna Bontemps called him that), Langston long ago wedded poetry and music in public sessions. In the early 1920s, in the homes of Harlem friends, he read poems to a jazz background, sometimes with Fats Waller at the piano. Later in that decade he gave a reading to music sung by the Princeton Glee Club. Kenneth Rexroth remembers that he and Langston arranged to read poetry to jazz in bohemian tearooms in Chicago —The Green Mask and The Dill Pickle and then in The Shadows on the South Side. In the 1950s there was a fresh burst of jazz readings, all the way from Greenwich Village spots to the San Francisco beat hangouts. In 1961 Langston published *Ask Your Mama: 12 Moods for Jazz.* The poems were written for the ear, as one voice of a jazz ensemble given directions on what to play through his notes in the margins.

This is the black voice of the 1960s, the Freedom Movement man, whether he lives in Harlem or Trinidad, the Congo or Mississippi. An even more passionate expression of it is found in Langston's 1967 volume *The Panther and the Lash*. Its seventy poems include some written as long ago as the early 1930s ("Christ in Alabama") and others, like "The Backlash Blues," in the last year of his life. The mood of the book is militant, angry, defiant. It is today's voice, yet much of it came out of experience suffered long ago. Perhaps the book, which appeared in July 1967 (two months after his death) was his way of saying to the young generation, I'm still here, by your side. The book—ignored by the critics—had a phenomenal success within the first few months, with over seven thousand copies sold in hardcover and paperback editions.

There are no nature poems or love lyrics in his last book, nor were there many in his earlier volumes. He did not care very much for the countryside. If friends got him out to a country home, he rarely went outdoors, and never wanted to take a walk or go for a swim. "I am as happy in the city in August as I am in the wilds—indeed, happier. I like wild people much better than I do wild animals," he said. If a collaboration required him to stay indefinitely in the country, he would usually find some excuse to go back to the city within a couple of weeks. He came from the small-town Midwest, but the city was his adopted and truer home. "Any city," he said, "any place where the animals are in zoos, the chickens in frozen-food bins, the birds keep the same hours as humans, and the lights burn all night long."

The conventional poet's beauty and lyricism were not for him. They were really related to another world, "to ivory towers, to your head in the clouds, feet floating off the earth. Unfortunately, having been born poor—and also colored—in Missouri, I was stuck in the mud from the beginning. Try as I might to float off into the clouds, poverty and Jim Crow would grab me by the heels, and right back on earth I would land. A third-floor furnished room is the nearest thing I have ever had to an ivory tower."

For him, as for most other black poets, the basic subject was freedom. No matter what forms Negro poetry has taken, the words are about freedom. Race, color, and the emotions related to them in a land that treats its black citizens like pariahs—how many Negro writers have been able to forget about them?

It was only natural, Langston believed, that Negro art is largely protest art. "Our time today is the time of color from Selma to Saigon, and of the heartaches and heartbreaks of racial conflict from Cape Town to Chicago." He was confirming in 1965 what Dr. Du Bois had predicted back in 1903: "The problem of the twentieth century is the problem of the color line."

To Langston's early poems can be traced the word that has lately come to mean so much to black Americans. "Soul." Look back at the refrain of "The Negro Speaks of Rivers"—

My soul has grown deep like the rivers.

It was the first time, Arna Bontemps has pointed out, that the word was used with the meaning it has for young Negroes today.

Alain Locke saw it in the young poet's work very early. He said in 1929: "The folk-lyrics of Langston Hughes have spontaneous moods and rhythms, and carry irresistible conviction. They are our really most successful efforts up to this date to recapture the folk-soul."

The word was used again in Langston's poem "My People"—

The night is beautiful
So the faces of my people.

The stars are beautiful
So the eyes of my people.

Beautiful, also, is the sun.
Beautiful, also, are the souls of my people.

Asked what "soul" meant to him, Langston answered, "a sort of synthesis of the essence of the Negro folk arts, particularly the old music and its flavor, expressed in contemporary ways but so clearly and emotionally colored with the old, that it gives a distinctly 'Negro' flavor to today's material in music, painting, writing, or merely in personal attitudes and conversation."

You can find "soul," he said, in such examples as Ray Charles' or Margaret Bonds' music, in Jacob Lawrence's paintings or in Alvin Ailey's ballets. There were overtones of it in the Harlem and Watts riots of the 1960s, things "that whites feel but fail to understand," he went on, "something to which only 'soul-brothers' born to the tradition can fully react in whatever form it occurs."

Langston Hughes' poetry has long been neglected by the dominant school of American literary criticism. Not all of his poetry, of course, deserves equal attention. Even at its best it was distant from the formal traditions the academic critics respect, and they chose to overlook it. Its seeming simplicity deceived them. They thought of him—when they noticed him at all—as only "an inspired reporter of the surface of things." Yet Kenneth Rexroth has observed that he was, "for an American, an extraordinarily sophisticated writer, which is probably why Americans took his apparent simplicity at its apparent face value. In France, where such striving for the greatest possible simplicity is common, his work was probably more accurately judged."

The neglect he suffered at the hands of the literary powers was not limited to himself alone. All Negro poets have been ignored by the makers of anthologies of American poetry. From time to time Langston publicly called attention to the fact that, to white anthologists, black writers were invisible. He pointed out that there was not a single black poet in *The Oxford Book of American Verse,* in *Modern Poetry,* in *The Pocket Book of American Poems,* in *100 American Poems,* in *A Complete College Reader,* in *Best Loved Poems,* in *An Anthology of American Verse,* in *Modern American Verse.*

A notable exception among anthologists was the poet Louis Untermeyer, who as early as 1928 included Dunbar, Cullen and Hughes in his collection of *Modern American and British Poetry,* widely used in the schools. But that was a long time ago. Addison Gayle, Jr., who as a high-school student had heard Hughes speak and who went on to become a college English teacher, observed after Hughes'

death that "the colleges of this country, their English departments in particular, which have exalted
Robert Burns, dismissed Hughes completely, utter-
ing their synonym for Negro writers: simple. . . .
His treatment by the academic establishment is the
best example of what it means to be a Negro writer
in America."

But Langston Hughes went on being a writer, a
black writer, he would say, not "just a writer," and
never afraid to use the material and the language of
his people. He knew that the local and the regional
can—and do—become universal. As with Burns or
O'Casey. To young Negro writers he said, "Do not
be afraid of yourselves. *You* are the world."

He left this world on May 22, 1967. He had
gone into Polyclinic Hospital in Manhattan on May
6, having waked in the night with some acute pain
he could not account for. There had been no signs of
illness, and his friends did not think anything was
seriously wrong. But day after day passed, and he
was still there, soon shut off from almost all contact
with the world outside. There was surgery for a
minor condition, and then he sank rapidly and unex-
pectedly. Chronic heart and kidney conditions he
had been unaware of or paid no attention to lessened

257

his chances. At ten-forty on Monday night, May 22, alone except for a nurse, he died.

The news, appearing on the front page of *The New York Times* the next morning, and in the press throughout the world, came as a great shock. Few had even known he was ill. So young and vital had he always seemed that none but his oldest friends realized he was in his sixty-sixth year. Nicolás Guillén, the Cuban poet, wrote what so many felt: "The truth is that I could expect anything from Langston except the fact that he might die."

The memorial service for him, held in Harlem a few days later, was packed with old friends. Even now, in death, his humor and toughness of spirit carried over. From *Shakespeare in Harlem* someone read the poem "Wake"—

> Tell all my mourners
> To mourn in red—
> Cause there ain't no sense
> In my bein' dead.

And at the very end, by Langston's own request, as a parting joke for his friends, a jazz trio played the old tune "Do Nothing Till You Hear from Me."

24 *Postscript*

No short biography of Langston Hughes can include everything he has done, every place he has been, everyone he has known, and every work he has written. The two volumes of his own autobiography (*The Big Sea* and *I Wonder As I Wander*) total 740 pages, but they brought him down only through 1937, when he had lived hardly half his years. And even these leave out a great deal.

The last half of his life saw an ever greater variety in his writing. The direction was always the same, however. "I document the feelings of our time in relation to myself and my own people, and, of course, the problems of our democracy," he told an interviewer in 1963.

"Feeling"—that is the heart of it. His work, no matter what form it took, rang with true feeling.

The man was his work, the work, the man. Saunders Redding has pointed this out:

"There is this difference between racial thought and feeling: what the professors, the ministers, the physicians, the social workers think, the domestics, the porters, the dock hands, the factory girls, and the streetwalkers feel—feel in a great tide that pours over into song and shout, prayer and cursing, laughter and tears. More than any other writer of his race, Langston Hughes has been swept with this tide of feeling."

Other Negro writers, such as Richard Wright, have paid tribute to Langston Hughes for opening the way to realism and honesty in Negro literature. He portrayed Negro life and interpreted it for countless people at home and abroad. Around the world he was heard as the voice of the American Negro, a designation that probably embarrassed him, for he knew that every writer speaks first for himself and himself alone. If he is aware and has the talent, he explores a range of values that reveal the humanity he shares with others.

It was his poems that first made him known, and it is still his poems that are the root of his reputation. But he ventured into many other forms of writing. Often he worked with composers, writing the book and lyrics for operas, musical folk comedies, and gospel shows. Both *Troubled Island,* with music by Jan Meyerowitz, and *Street Scene,* whose score was composed by Kurt Weill, have been presented by the New York City Opera as well as other companies, and *Simply Heavenly,* starring Jesse B. Semple, was popular both off-Broadway and on. His *Black Nativity* played at the Festival in Spoleto, Italy, in 1962, toured Europe for a year, and then played Christmas week of 1963 at Philharmonic Hall in Lincoln Center, New York. He wrote more than twenty plays, operas, musicals, and gospel pieces.

He made many contributions to the popularizing of Negro history, with books designed for adults and for young people. Standard volumes in their fields are *A Pictorial History of the Negro in America* and *Black Magic: A Pictorial History of the Negro in American Entertainment* (both done in collaboration with Milton Meltzer). His *Fight for Freedom* is the story of the NAACP.

In 1952 he began writing for young readers, and in the next eight years produced many books on Negro heroes, on Negro musicians, on jazz, on rhythms, on the West Indies, on Africa. He was surprised to discover how successful these were. When the first title went rapidly into a second printing he voiced his delight to an editor at Knopf. Perhaps I should have turned to this long ago, he wrote. But Knopf, who did not publish his children's books, stuck loyally by him all through the years. It took twenty-five years for *The Weary Blues,* his first book of poems, to sell seven thousand copies. *Fine Clothes,* the second, had sold only two thousand between 1927 and 1942, when the plates were melted down during wartime. *Shakespeare in Harlem, Fields of Wonder, One Way Ticket,* his poems of the 1940s, sold from two to five thousand copies. This was common for most poets, black or white. But even *The Big Sea,* so enthusiastically reviewed, had sold only five thousand copies in its first ten years. And *I Wonder As I Wander,* the second volume of his autobiography, took two years to sell three thousand copies.

With Arna Bontemps he produced two anthologies, *The Poetry of the Negro* and *The Book of Negro Folklore.* By himself he edited *An African Treasury, The Book of Negro Humor, New Negro Poets: U.S.A.,* and *The Best Short Stories by Negro Writers.*

His own work has been gathered into several large volumes: *Selected Poems by Langston Hughes, Five Plays by Langston Hughes, The Langston Hughes Reader,* and *The Best of Simple.*

Besides his frequent lecture tours, in which he often spoke to school and college audiences, he gave special time to teaching. In 1947 he taught creative writing for a semester at Atlanta University and two years later worked with children as poet in residence at the Laboratory School of the University of Chicago.

In his long career he earned many honors, from the first *Opportunity* prize when he was twenty-three to his election in 1961 to the highest honor an American artist can earn, membership in the American Academy of Arts and Letters. Lincoln University, Howard University, and Western Reserve University gave him their honorary degree of doctor of literature. He received Guggenheim and Rosenwald fellowships and an American Academy of Arts and Letters grant. Both the Anisfield-Wolfe Award and the Spingarn Medal for contributions to interracial understanding were given to him. The Free Academy of Arts in Hamburg honored him in 1964 and Emperor Haile Selassie of Ethiopia decorated him in 1966.

Many times he was invited to take part in festivals of music, poetry, or the arts here and abroad, from the Stratford Festival in Canada to the Berliner Festwochen, from the Newport Jazz Festival in Rhode Island to the World Festival of Negro Arts in Dakar, Senegal.

It sounds like a life of great fun, and it was. But it was also a life of hardship and many frustrations. Unlike some other writers, Langston never had his way eased by a financial lucky strike. None of his work ever swept in the great profits of a best seller, or sold to Hollywood at high prices, or was a smash hit on Broadway.

Yet he lived as generously as if it had. He gave away so many copies of his own books that some recipients mistakenly thought he got them for nothing. He was thoughtful and considerate of friends, remembering birthdays and anniversaries, bestowing gifts upon their children, concerned when they were ill or in trouble, glad with them when things were going well. His postcards and notes streamed out in that flowing green ink to friends all over the world no matter where he himself might be, in Dakar or Detroit. And always the messages showed an awareness of the friend as an individual

—a private joke, a specially made-up rhyme, a reminder of something shared in common, a promise of things to come. He was the kind of man who could even nurture an enduring friendship through the mails with someone he never saw, a friendship that went on for twenty years until death ended it.

Perhaps his great gift for friendship was that, as one poet put it, "he never forgot he was living in enemy country and wanted to make common cause with his friends, black and white."

He was a true professional in his relations with editors. Maria Leiper of Simon and Schuster said of him, "I never had a pleasanter or more rewarding relationship with any of the writers I worked with over almost thirty years. He was unfailingly cooperative, thoughtful, dependable: if he said a chapter would be in by a Monday, it was there at 9 A.M. He gave careful attention to any suggestions made, he was flexible, sensitive, enormously helpful with promotion and selling. He was one of the hardest-working individuals I've ever known. Nevertheless, he was tolerant when other less conscientious, energetic, or efficient people were concerned. When they made mistakes, he was understanding and forgiving."

He was generous "beyond any reasonable measure," as one young poet said, in what he did for
other writers. Judith Jones at Knopf said he was always calling up to suggest she might want to see the
work of some young poet or novelist he thought
good. Julian Mayfield wrote that few black writers
of his generation failed to use Langston as a reference for a fellowship or foundation grant. He even
handed on to them assignments he might well have
done himself, because he knew they needed the
money and the recognition. Unlike many other writers, with whom ego is uppermost, he did not thrust
himself forward so as to keep others back. Of course
the encouragement he gave others meant he was
flooded with requests for help, both literary and financial. For a writer who worked so hard himself it
must have been a huge burden, but he never spoke
of it.

Near his front door on 127th Street he grew ivy.
It was the only green thing on that Harlem block,
said Julia Fields, one of the young writers he encouraged. "And now I think," she wrote after his
death, "who will grow the ivy or see that it is there?
We younger poets are in turn the budding new
green of his ivy."

Author's Note and Acknowledgments

I met Langston Hughes in 1955, when we began collaboration on a history book. It was early in 1967, just as we were finishing work on our second book together, that I asked whether he would mind if I tried to write a short biography of him. He gave me his permission, supplied material from his files, and answered many of my questions. I was working on the book when his sudden death occurred.

This book is in no sense an official biography. Langston saw some of it in early draft, but did not try to set any limits on what to include or how it should be written. After his death my research continued, and was considerably extended, but with one important limitation. Access to the Hughes papers in the James Weldon Johnson Collection of the Yale University Library, which I had referred to earlier, was now cut off by the literary executors of the estate.

My first thanks for the considerable help given to me in this book are owed to Raoul Abdul, who was friend and assistant to Langston Hughes for many years, and to the staff at Lincoln University in Pennsylvania, and the Schomburg Collection of the New York Public Library. A great many other people who knew Langston Hughes over the years were very generous in permitting interviews, writing me in answer to questions, lending me letters, papers, photos, and clippings. I owe much to them for their recollections, their insights, and their encouragement. (The responsibility for the book, of course, is entirely mine.) I name them here with special thanks:

Samuel W. Allen, Eubie Blake, Arna Bontemps, Gwendolyn Brooks, Anthony Buttitta, Walt and Rose Carmon, Vinette Carroll, Helen Chesnutt, John P. Davis, Frances Drucker, Ethel Ellis, Alfred Farrell, Franklin Folsom, Lawrence Gellert, Byron S. Greenberg, Jerome Gross, Eugene C. Holmes, Hermie Huiswoud, Jean Blackwell Hutson, Russell and Rowena Jelliffe, Judith Jones, Ernest Kaiser, Hajime Kijima, William Koshland, Henry Kraus, Paul Kuehner, Russel Lampus, Ben Lehman.

Also Maria Leiper, Florence Becker Lennon, Theophilus Lewis, Margaret Marshall, Daniel F. Meckes, August Meier, Loren Miller, Mollie Moon, Joseph North, Louise Thompson Patterson, Bernard Perry, Rosey E. Pool, Kenneth Rexroth, Yvette Ripplinger, Pauline G. Schindler, Joshua Shelley, Walter P. Sheppard, Elie and Hannah Siegmeister, Noble Sissle, Bernard Smith, Amy Spingarn, Arthur B. Spingarn, Ivan von Auw, Emery Wimbish, Ella Winter, Fritz T. Wurzmann, Samuel Yellen.

Bibliography

The most important source of published information for this biography was of course the works of Langston Hughes, especially the two volumes of his autobiography, and the files of his newspaper columns, which appeared weekly for over twenty years in the Chicago *Defender* and later also in the New York *Post*. Most of his unpublished letters and papers are on deposit in the James Weldon Johnson Memorial Collection at the Yale University Library. Other material is in the Schomburg Collection of the New York Public Library, and the library at Lincoln University, Pennsylvania. References to other newspaper and periodical pieces, by or about Langston Hughes, are too numerous to list.

Bibliography

WORKS BY LANGSTON HUGHES

POEMS

The Weary Blues. New York: Knopf, 1926.
Fine Clothes to the Jew. New York: Knopf, 1927.
Dear Lovely Death. Amenia, New York: Troutbeck Press, 1931.
The Dream Keeper. New York: Knopf, 1932.
Shakespeare in Harlem. New York: Knopf, 1942.
Fields of Wonder. New York: Knopf, 1947.
One-Way Ticket. New York: Knopf, 1949.
Montage of a Dream Deferred. New York: Holt, 1951.
Selected Poems of Langston Hughes. New York: Knopf, 1959.
Ask Your Mama. New York: Knopf, 1961.
The Panther and the Lash. New York: Knopf, 1967.

SHORT STORIES

The Ways of White Folks. New York: Knopf, 1934.
Laughing to Keep from Crying. New York: Holt, 1952.
Something in Common and Other Stories. New York: Hill and Wang, 1963.

NOVELS

Not Without Laughter. New York: Knopf, 1930.
Tambourines to Glory. New York: John Day, 1959.

SIMPLE BOOKS

Simple Speaks His Mind. New York: Simon and Schuster, 1950.
Simple Takes a Wife. New York: Simon and Schuster, 1953.

Simple Stakes a Claim. New York: Rinehart, 1957.

The Best of Simple. New York: Hill and Wang, 1961.

Simple's Uncle Sam. New York: Hill and Wang, 1965.

AUTOBIOGRAPHY

The Big Sea. New York: Knopf, 1940. Reprinted by Hill and Wang, 1963.

I Wonder As I Wander. New York: Rinehart, 1956. Reprinted by Hill and Wang, 1964.

PLAYS

Five Plays by Langston Hughes. (Included are *Mulatto, Soul Gone Home, Little Ham, Simply Heavenly,* and *Tambourines to Glory.*) Edited by Webster Smalley. Bloomington: Indiana University Press, 1963.

HISTORY

A Pictorial History of the Negro in America. Co-author with Milton Meltzer. New York: Crown, 1956. Revised Edition, 1963.

Fight for Freedom: The Story of the NAACP. New York: Berkeley, 1962.

Black Magic: A Pictorial History of the Negro in American Entertainment. Co-author with Milton Meltzer. Englewood Cliffs, N.J.: Prentice-Hall, 1967.

BOOKS FOR YOUNG READERS

The First Book of Negroes. New York: Franklin Watts, 1952.

Famous American Negroes. New York: Dodd, Mead, 1954.

The First Book of Rhythms. New York: Franklin Watts, 1954.

Famous Negro Music Makers. New York: Dodd, Mead, 1955.

The First Book of Jazz. New York: Franklin Watts, 1955.

The First Book of the West Indies. New York: Franklin Watts, 1956.

Famous Negro Heroes of America. New York: Dodd, Mead, 1958.

The First Book of Africa. New York: Franklin Watts, 1960.

ANTHOLOGIES EDITED BY LANGSTON HUGHES

The Poetry of the Negro 1746–1949. Co-editor with Arna Bontemps. Garden City, N.Y.: Doubleday, 1949.

The Langston Hughes Reader. New York: Braziller, 1958.

The Book of Negro Folklore. Co-editor with Arna Bontemps. New York: Dodd, Mead, 1958.

An African Treasury. New York: Crown, 1960.

Poems from Black Africa. Bloomington: Indiana University Press, 1963.

New Negro Poets: U.S.A. Bloomington: Indiana University Press, 1964.

The Book of Negro Humor. New York: Dodd, Mead, 1966.

The Best Short Stories by Negro Writers. Boston: Little, Brown, 1967.

MISCELLANEOUS

The Sweet Flypaper of Life. Text by Hughes, photographs by Roy De Carava. New York: Simon and Schuster, 1955. Reprinted by Hill and Wang, 1967.

TRANSLATIONS BY LANGSTON HUGHES

Masters of the Dew. By Jacques Roumains. Translated with Mercer Cook. New York: Reynal and Hitchcock, 1947.

Cuba Libre. By Nicolas Guillen. Translated with Ben Frederic Carruthers. Los Angeles: Ward Ritchie Press, 1948.

Romancero Gitano. By Federico García Lorca. Published by Beloit Poetry Journal, 1951.

Selected Poems of Gabriela Mistral. Bloomington: Indiana University Press, 1957.

RECORDINGS OF LANGSTON HUGHES' WORK

Simply Heavenly. Musical. By the cast. Columbia, OL 5240.

Street Scene. Musical. By the cast. Columbia, OL 4139.

Jericho Jim Crow. Musical. By the cast. Folkways, FL 9671.

The Weary Blues. Poems read by the author with jazz background by Charlie Mingus and Henry Red Allen. Verve, VSP 36.

The Dream Keeper. Poems read by the author. Folkways, FP 104.

The Glory of Negro History. Narrated by the author. Folkways, FP 752.

The Story of Jazz. Narrated by the author. Folkways, FP 712.

Rhythms of the World. Narrated by the author. Folkways, FP 740.

The Best of Simple. Stories read by Melvin Stewart. Folkways, FL 9789.

Did You Ever Hear the Blues? Songs sung by Big Miller. United Artists, UAL 3047.

BOOKS ABOUT LANGSTON HUGHES

Langston Hughes. By François Dodat. Paris: Postes Twayne, 1967.

Langston Hughes. By François Dodat. Paris: Postes d'aujourd'hui Series, Editions Seghers, 1964.

Langston Hughes ou L'Étoile Noire. By Raymond Quinot. Éditions Bruxelles, 1964.

A Bio-Bibliography of Langston Hughes. By Donald Dickinson. Hamden, Connecticut: Shoe String Press, 1967.

Index

ABOUT THE AUTHOR

Milton Meltzer's friendship with Langston Hughes began when they collaborated on *A Pictorial History of the Negro in America,* which was published in 1956. Their second pictorial history, *Black Magic,* dealing with the Negro in American entertainment, appeared in 1967. Mr. Meltzer has also written biographies of three nine-teenth-century antislavery figures: *A Light in the Dark: The Life of Samuel Gridley Howe; Tongue of Flame: The Life of Lydia Maria Child;* and *Thaddeus Stevens and the Fight for Negro Rights.* He edited the award-winning *In Their Own Words,* a three-volume documentary history of the American Negro. In addition he has written for magazines, newpapers, radio, television, and documentary films.

Mr. Meltzer was born in Worcester, Massachusetts, and educated at Columbia University. He and his wife live in New York. They have two daughters.